Early praise for *Creating Great Teams: How Self-Selection Lets People Excel*

Teams are the fuel that powers the agile engine. In this book Sandy and David explore self-selection, a process that helps professionals organize themselves into effective teams. The detailed descriptions of the why and how of self-selection and the many examples make this a very useful book. I highly recommend it!

➤ **Ben Linders**
   Independent consultant in agile, lean, quality, and continuous improvement

This is dynamite! I now realize how much I wish I had had a book like this earlier. It provides a hands-on path on how to harness people's motivation through self-selection! I read it in just one go. Nice structure. Great language. Concrete. Inspiring. Love it!

➤ **Jimmy Janlén**
   Agile coach, Crisp and Nomad8

I've believed for a long time in the power of self-selection, so I am excited that there is finally a handbook on how to go about it. Sandy and David give concrete advice on facilitating self-selection within an organization and what to look out for. Anyone reading this book will feel prepared to embark on what otherwise might seem like a very scary journey. I will definitely recommend it to coaches and organizations I work with.

➤ **Karen Greaves**
   Agile coach and trainer, Growing Agile

I love this book! I've wondered about self-selection and how I might do it. I usually ask teams to self-select, but very simply and only with two teams. This book has provided me with step-by-step guidelines on how to scale my approach. I particularly love the section on what you should do before a self-selection event—an often overlooked part.

➤ **Samantha Laing**
  Agile coach, Growing Agile

In *Creating Great Teams*, you'll find guidance for building your strongest teams through self-selection. For most managers, it's a leap of faith, and the authors ensure a softer landing. They describe their experiences with self-selection in detail. You follow along with helpful checklists. In the end, you learn to trust that you will have the right people focused on the right work. I'm a fan of great liftoff activities for teams, and this one is outstanding. The self-selection process prepares people to do their best work and stay engaged. I look forward to sharing this book with managers and team leaders.

➤ **Diana Larson**
  Consultant, speaker, and co-author of *Liftoff: Launching Agile Teams and Projects* and *Agile Retrospectives: Making Good Teams Great*

Creating Great Teams

How Self-Selection Lets People Excel

Sandy Mamoli
David Mole

The Pragmatic Bookshelf

Dallas, Texas • Raleigh, North Carolina

Many of the designations used by manufacturers and sellers to distinguish their products are claimed as trademarks. Where those designations appear in this book, and The Pragmatic Programmers, LLC was aware of a trademark claim, the designations have been printed in initial capital letters or in all capitals. The Pragmatic Starter Kit, The Pragmatic Programmer, Pragmatic Programming, Pragmatic Bookshelf, PragProg and the linking *g* device are trademarks of The Pragmatic Programmers, LLC.

Every precaution was taken in the preparation of this book. However, the publisher assumes no responsibility for errors or omissions, or for damages that may result from the use of information (including program listings) contained herein.

Our Pragmatic courses, workshops, and other products can help you and your team create better software and have more fun. For more information, as well as the latest Pragmatic titles, please visit us at *https://pragprog.com*.

The team that produced this book includes:

Katharine Dvorak (editor)
Linda Recktenwald (copyedit)
Dave Thomas (layout)
Janet Furlow (producer)
Ellie Callahan (support)

For international rights, please contact *rights@pragprog.com*.

Printed in the United States of America.
ISBN-13: 978-1-68050-128-5
Printed on acid-free paper.
Book version: P1.0—November 2015

Contents

Acknowledgments

Many people have contributed to this book and we'd like to say thank you to all of them!

Thank you to Julie Starr for cleaning up our language and helping us structure our thoughts; Brenda Leeuwenberg for asking difficult questions, pointing out holes and inconsistencies, and constantly challenging us; Paula Boock for pointing out what publishers actually do and making us contact The Pragmatic Bookshelf; and our editor, Katharine Dvorak, for her inspired and sane advice, her lightning speed, and her awesome editing.

Thank you also to Susannah Pfalzer, Dave Thomas, and Andy Hunt at The Pragmatic Bookshelf and all of the reviewers: Alessandro Bahgat, Jacob Chae, Derek Graham, Alexander Henry, Aaron Kalair, Nigel Lowry, Matthew Margolis, Loren Sands-Ramshaw, Tibor Simic, Federico Tomassetti, and Colin Yates.

A special thank you goes to Trade Me, which trusted its employees to solve a complex problem and let us write about it.

Foreword

As a consultant and expert in organizational dynamics, I've worked with scores of organizations, and over the course of four decades, I've observed hundreds of teams and team formations. In many of those cases, the focus was assembling the required mix of technical skills—as if the skills existed apart from the people who had them.

Many years ago, I worked for a big, multinational corporation. The company had technology centers spread over every time zone. Every possible skill was represented somewhere in the company. "Couldn't we save money and avoid hiring new people if we could make efficient use of those resources?" an executive wondered.

Every technical employee filled out a profile and became an entry in what was called the Global Skills Inventory (GSI) database. When the executives approved a new initiative, a manager created a skills list and cranked up the database. The manager fed in the requirements and—boom!—the GSI spit out a list of "resources" deployed for the project "team."

It's easy to see the faulty reasoning behind the GSI database. People are not interchangeable units, and technical skills are only part of the equation when people need to work collaboratively.

But what about the traditional way, relying on management judgment to form teams? I've seen selection processes range from very informal—what my friend and fellow agile coach Don Gray calls the Five You's Method ("You, you, you, you, and you. You're the team.")—to very formal processes with job analysis, selection criteria, interviews, testing, and auditions.

Even with the most rigorous process—and in spite of managers' good intentions—the likelihood that any group of people actually gels and becomes a team is low. A few teams soar, many more slog along, and most don't show the level of responsibility and engagement managers hope for.

Fundamentally, two factors determine whether a group will forge itself into a team:

- Do these people want to work on this problem?

- Do these people want to work with each other?

Neither a computer program nor a manager can answer these questions. Only the employees who will do the work can. And that's the subject of this lovely and useful book.

Some managers worry that given the option to self-select, people will act like high-school kids and choose people they like and work that appeals to them. Yes, people may choose those they like to work with on work that seems interesting. That seems sensible to me. People work best when they have choice over what they work on and who they work with. Managers worry that some work won't be chosen—failing to account for employees who will do less-than-thrilling work because they understand that it's necessary for continued operations and place high value on that.

Managers want engaged teams who take responsibility and show initiative. But these concerns hint at a contradiction: a belief that employees won't make responsible decisions left to choose their own teams. Management selection for teams actually works against team responsibility by communicating that people aren't capable of making responsible choices about work and coworkers. However, when teams self-select they're much more invested in success. Team self-selection creates the conditions for team engagement and responsibility.

How do you go from managerial selection to self-selection? If your only image is chaos or choosing up sides for sports—it makes sense that team self-selection looks like a dubious undertaking. It's not as simple as putting everyone in big room and letting them mill around until they find a group they like. As Sandy and David explain, thought and preparation are required for successful team self-selection. This book shows you step by step what successful team self-selection looks like. It provides enough detail so many more managers can imagine how trying team self-selection might look and feel in their own organization.

Sandy and David's book is radical in that it upends the traditional role managers have in hiring and selecting people for teams. It's utterly un-radical in that it shows a practical way forward—based on what researchers have known for years:

- People want to do a good job and contribute to their customers and companies

- Employees work best when they have choice

- They take more responsibility for their own decisions than those made by others

- Collaborative work depends on relationships

- When you treat people like adults, they act that way

Managers need to paint the vision of what needs to be done, organize the work in a sensible way, identify constraints, and then let employees choose their own teams.

This book will help many managers realize that the opposite of managerial team selection isn't chaos. It's commitment, creativity, and engagement, which is what they've been searching for all along.

Esther Derby

Co-author of *Agile Retrospectives: Making Good Teams Great* and *Behind Closed Doors: Secrets of Great Management*

November 2015

Introduction: Self-Selection and Why You Should Care

Fast growth has a way of forcing organizational change on a business, but it also presents opportunities to try new ways of working. When Trade Me, one of New Zealand's biggest ecommerce providers, hit a new level of growth, we saw an opportunity to drive productivity by reorganizing the company into small, stable agile teams.

We found the best way to do it was using self-selection: trust the people who work in the organization—the engineers, testers, business analysts, designers, user experience professionals, and product owners—to come up with the best way to structure their teams. It seemed radical when we started, but it worked. Removing the managers from the equation and trusting in the employees involved created a fascinating story and incredible outcomes for everyone.

What Is Self-Selection?

Self-selection is a facilitated process of letting people self-organize into small, cross-functional teams. Based on the belief that people are at their happiest and most productive if they can choose what they work on and who they work with, we think it's the fastest and most efficient way to form stable teams.

To avoid confusion, we're not referring here to self-organizing teams. *Self-organizing teams* are groups of motivated individuals who work together toward a shared goal and have the ability and authority to take decisions and readily adapt to changing demands. We like self-organizing teams, but that's not what this book is about.

This book is about self-selection, which is a process you can use to set up self-organizing teams in the first place. Self-selection happens at an organizational level rather than at a team level and is a way to get everyone into teams. Another term for a self-selected team is a *self-designed team.*

Why Should You Care?

If you work in an industry that benefits from people working in small, cross-functional teams, then this book is for you.

If you are a CEO, CTO, head of projects, VP of engineering, agile coach, head of marketing, or any other kind of manager who wants to structure your organization or department into small teams, you will learn why self-selection is the fastest and safest way to do so. You will learn how to prepare for and organize a self-selection event, how to convince your fellow managers that it's a good idea in the first place, and how to communicate with your self-selection participants to make sure everyone is on board and ready.

If you are a team member, developer, tester, UX designer, or business analyst, you will read about what it feels like to be part of a self-selection process and what the consequences are for your daily work. You will learn how to influence your colleagues and your bosses to be open to the idea of self-selection. You will be able to provide your boss with a plan for how to facilitate a self-selection event and evidence that the system works.

This book describes a process that will work whether you need to form teams from scratch, want to improve the design of existing teams, or are on the verge of a big team reshuffle. How do you know that the teams in your organization represent the best possible combinations of people? How do you know that everyone is working in the team they would like to work in? There's only one way to find out: ask them; then let them decide. By giving your staff choice through self-selection, you allow them to establish the best designed teams, and you will get the most out of your company.

Self-selection is a great way to get going if you don't have fixed teams yet or to revitalize people if you feel your organization or teams are stuck in a rut.

We've seen self-selection work time and time again with teams building software, websites, and apps, but we've also found that these principles translate to other industries and fields where people can or should work in small teams, such as marketing, sales, human resources, and even finance.

We've Done It, and So Can You

Our first trial self-selection event was in October 2013 at Trade Me, one of New Zealand's biggest ecommerce providers. Since then we've run the largest self-selection process we know of and repeated the process many times across multiple locations. Many more companies have since used our ideas and processes to run self-selection events across the world.

In this book we share a case study of how we used self-selection to decide on the structure and composition of twenty-two new agile teams across Trade Me's technology department—a process that involved more than 150 people. We also demonstrate and explain a repeatable process for facilitating a self-selection event at scale.

Our aim is to convince you that self-selection is not only valid but also highly rewarding and can be a successful and positive approach for all kinds of organizations.

Who Are We?

We're Sandy Mamoli and David Mole, and we spent several years doing transformational work with Trade Me. If you aren't from New Zealand (or Australia at a stretch), then the chances are you will not have heard of the company we're talking about. Trade Me is an iconic Kiwi brand with more than 3.7 million accounts, and more than a million New Zealanders will have bought or sold something via the site in the past year.

The site is a popular place for Kiwis to buy, sell, and trade everything from cars and antiques to clothes, crafts, property, and farm gear. It's a Kiwi success story, having grown over the past sixteen years to a unique position where it commands more than half of New Zealand's domestic Internet traffic, serving more than one *billion* pages per month. For context, there are only 4.5 million people living in New Zealand, a country with Internet penetration up around 86%.

Trade Me has also been growing pretty fast. A year ago there were 110 employees in their technology department; now there are approximately 250. In total, there are more than 450 staff members at the time of writing and no sign of the growth slowing down anytime soon.

What Problem Did We Need to Solve?

The organization had reached a point where the technology department was increasing in size by roughly one person a week, but they noticed that adding new people no longer meant they were getting more done; if anything, the speed of delivery was actually slowing down. At the time people weren't organized into fixed teams; rather, the teams were assembled at the start of a project and disassembled when the project ended. Employees were not dedicated to a team or project; their time was split into percentages and their assignments were determined by their manager.

Over the course of time a web of dependencies had evolved whereby every person and project were reliant on someone else, and there were always a significant number of handovers and delays between groups of people. Projects were constantly being paused and put on hold because there was no one available to work on them; everyone was busy somewhere else. No one had an overview of the people and the projects, so there was no big picture of what was happening.

Sound familiar?

We wanted to avoid the delays caused by waiting for staff to be freed from other projects, and we wanted to minimize handovers with their associated loss of tacit knowledge. Our strategy was to pull people out of this complex matrix and move them into fixed, stable teams where we could ensure that one person would work on only one team, and one team would work on only one project at any time. (Note that we use the term *project*, but technically it was more of a value stream or initiative, as there frequently was no hard start or end date.)

So, let's get started. In the first chapter we dive into what a stable team design looks like and why it's so important. Then we break down the process we took to guide Trade Me through a self-selection event, beginning with how we created the right context and ending with how we facilitated it toward a successful outcome. (While we discuss Trade Me's self-selection success story, this book was a completely independent project and not affiliated with or associated with Trade Me in any way.)

CHAPTER 1

The Art of Stable Team Design

"Brazil has Neymar. Argentina has Messi. Portugal has Ronaldo. Germany has a team!" This tweet from a soccer fan flew around the world following Germany's surprising defeat of host country Brazil 7:1 in the 2014 World Cup semifinals. Germany went on to claim the title of world champions, a success that experts attribute to a football culture based on team spirit and shared long-term goals, a culture that relies on players who fit the team rather than individual superstars.

Germany was far from having the greatest individual players in the world in 2014, but it did have the highest performing team.

As former English footballer Michael Owen stated in *The Telegraph*[1] following the match, "I once asked my good friend Didi Hamann what he considered the biggest difference between German and English football. He defined it to me as follows: 'If an English player is booked in a World Cup semi-final, and it means he can't play in the final, he starts crying on the pitch (as demonstrated by Paul Gascoigne in 1990),' said Didi. 'If it happens to a German, he puts it out of his mind and then scores the winning goal. One player is thinking about himself and the other his team.'"

In defeating Brazil, the German team demonstrated perfectly the triumph of a team mentality over individual needs. This applies to all kinds of teams.

Today's Work Demands Stable Teams

In software development, stable teams are higher performing and more productive. Research by Rally Software showed an almost 2:1 difference in throughput between software development teams that were 95% or more

---

1. http://www.telegraph.co.uk/sport/football/teams/germany/10962088/World-Cup-2014-Why-selfish-England-must-learn-from-selfless-Germany.html

dedicated compared with teams that were 50% or less dedicated. The 2014 white paper "The Impact of Agile Quantified,"[2] based on the analysis of the process and performance data of nearly 10,000 teams, indicated that stable agile teams result in up to 60% higher productivity.

One reason for greater productivity in stable teams is that they don't have to repeatedly go through the team-building stages of forming, storming, norming, and performing over and over again. Constantly changing and churning teams (as you often get when assembling and disassembling specific project teams) may never get out of the initial forming stage, and they could forever stay a group of individuals, no matter how talented.

Stable teams are more productive.

People working in small, stable teams are also happier. Certainly our own internal surveys showed that job satisfaction increased when we started working in fixed teams. Some of the responses highlighted that people felt more productive while working fewer hours and that being allocated 100% to one team reduced stress. We gained confidence from these comments coming at a time when our measurements demonstrated that overall productivity was also significantly increasing.

The Need for Speed

Some companies, especially those organizations founded during the Internet age, are born agile. They start out with small, cross-functional teams and scale by adding more teams as they grow.

But what about the rest of us? How do companies that are organized in a more traditional way move toward a small-team structure without descending into chaos or wasting valuable time? We have observed many organizations facing this challenge when they needed to accommodate rapid growth, started an agile adoption, or simply wanted to reorganize their existing teams because they felt they were in a rut.

When we first started moving toward stable teams at Trade Me, it was on quite a small scale, introducing one team at a time in a controlled manner. But as the company grew ever faster, we realized we were going to have to be able to scale up—and quickly.

We knew what we wanted: small, cross-functional teams that would persist over time and across projects. We'd seen measurable benefits in the initial

---

2.   https://www.rallydev.com/finally-get-real-data-about-benefits-adopting-agile?nid=6201

teams and knew we wanted to extend the stable approach right across the organization.

The impetus was also growing internally, as employees were seeing what was going on and starting to express their desire to be part of this new way of working. They could see how much other people enjoyed working in fixed teams, how much more fun their colleagues had (visibly and audibly across the office), and how much more they were achieving. Having some people work in a way that was so obviously a success and telling others they had to wait their turn seemed a little like we were treating some employees as second-class citizens.

To us it began to feel like a meaningless and frustrating delay. The controlled approach may have been vital initially, but we soon realized we had to go all in and move everyone into small, stable teams as quickly as we could.

We were deeply inspired by the workflow of the music-streaming service Spotify and its terminology of squads, chapters, and tribes. We also admired its culture, which promoted autonomy, mastery, and purpose. In their 2012 whitepaper "Scaling Agile @ Spotify with Tribes, Squads, Chapters & Guilds,"[3] Anders Ivarsson and Henrik Kniberg describe Spotify's culture and how the company is organized. The following image from this paper illustrates Spotify's squad, chapter, tribe, and guild concepts.

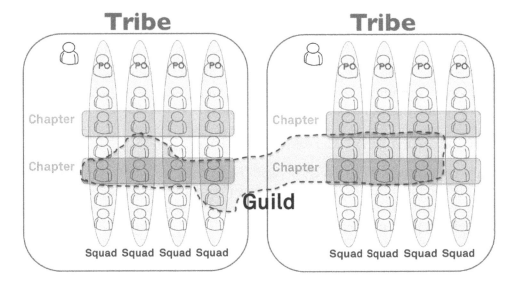

---

3. http://blog.crisp.se/2012/11/14/henrikkniberg/scaling-agile-at-spotify

At the core of Spotify's workflow is the *squad*; a small, cross-functional team whose members sit together and collectively possess all the skills required to design, develop, test, and release software. Squads are self-organizing and in full control of the processes and tools that help them achieve their goals. They are created with a strong purpose and are designed to feel like a mini-startup. In this book we'll use the term *squad* to represent the cross-functional teams we established at Trade Me.

A *tribe* is a collection of squads that work in related areas and can be seen as a kind of incubator for the squad mini-startups. Tribes have a fair degree of freedom and autonomy and are sized around the concept of *Dunbar's number*, which states that people cannot maintain a social relationship with more than 150 people.

The purpose of chapters and guilds is to share knowledge and tools. A *chapter* is a small group of people within a tribe who have similar skills and work within the same general competency area, such as testing, web development, or databases. Each chapter meets regularly to discuss their area of expertise and their specific challenges.

A *guild* is a more organic and wide-reaching community of common interests. Examples include the test-automation and agile coaching guild. Guilds reach across tribes, and anyone who is interested is welcome to join.

Squads are the vertical dimension of the matrix and, as people sit together and work toward a shared goal on a daily basis, considered their primary home. The horizontal dimension (chapter) is for sharing knowledge and tools and, while important, is secondary to the core concept of the squad.

With that inspiration, and our increasing sense of urgency, our next move was to come up with a plan for our next steps.

The Science Behind Team Design

Our vision was to have everyone working in a squad within the next three months, which meant finding the best way to run a squadification process—the term we came up with to describe the process whereby people select who is going to be part of which squad.

We started looking into the science behind the design of teams, which some research suggests is the most important factor in overall team performance. Studies conducted by J. Richard Hackman,[4] for example, found 60% of the

---

4.   http://www.estherderby.com/2011/11/miss-the-start-miss-the-end.html

variation in team effectiveness is attributable to the design of the team, 30% to the way the team is launched, and 10% to leader coaching once the team is under way.

This is certainly consistent with our own observations: we've seen more than one star-studded team grossly underperform because the mix of personalities just wasn't right. We've seen teams fail because the star players weren't able to see past their personal differences and were more focused on their own performance or objectives than the team's achievements.

We firmly believe that designing a team doesn't necessarily mean picking the best people but rather deciding on the best combination of people based on their interdependent skills, preferences, and personalities.

We knew we'd have to be considerate in our approach at Trade Me. Imagine if your manager or coach came to you and said, "Let's talk about your team and the way you work and potentially change everything from the ground up." That's a very important conversation to have in the right way. We knew that if we got it wrong we were going to annoy and worry a lot of people.

We looked at two potential methods for designing teams:

Managerial selection:
Managers decide on which team a person should work.

Self-selection:
People decide for themselves on which team they want to work.

Managerial Selection Breaks When Organizations Grow

Managerial selection is the traditional way of allocating people to teams. Good managers design teams based on their knowledge of employees' skills and personalities and who they think would get along with whom.

In a small company this often works well—a good manager is aware of relationships between people and knows the skills, personalities, and preferences of each of them. Often they come up with team compositions that are mostly right, and it's a quick way to get team selection done.

This model breaks down when a company grows or goes through a period of significant change, such as during an agile adoption. Managers might still know their direct reports' skills and personalities, but it becomes increasingly difficult to understand the intricacies of relationships among people as the number of relationships increases almost exponentially. In our experience the breaking point is around ten people.

As David remembers:

> *I would come out of meeting after meeting of managers where we would select staff for teams or projects based on our best guess. I remember so many conversations that started, "So, what squad is Peter going to be in?" "Peter is going to go into this squad."*

> *And then I'd have a conversation with Peter's manager or someone else who knew him and they'd say, "Oh, I think he really wants to work on this other part of the code," or "I've heard he doesn't like working with one of the people there," so we'd go back to the drawing board.*

> *We spent hour after hour as managers trying to unravel these scenarios (surprisingly, in hindsight, never actually talking directly to the person in question), and more often than not we'd get it wrong. We had a feeling something wasn't quite right with the way we were doing things, but at the same time it seemed so convention-ally sound. It's what managers do, right? They tell their staff what to work on. But something felt fundamentally wrong about the way we were going about it.*

When you think about it, managerial selection made good sense in its historical context of industrial factories where workers' tasks were relatively simple and repetitive, and workers were pretty much interchangeable. It simply didn't matter who worked with whom, and high-performing teams couldn't achieve anything a collection of people couldn't get done. In the complex and collaborative workflows of organizations today, however, managerial selection makes much less sense, but our methods haven't kept pace with the amount of change the working environment has gone through.

The same is true of the carrot-and-stick approach to motivating staff, which suggests that people charged with repetitive and boring tasks were best incentivized by monetary rewards. Author Daniel Pink turned the tables on that idea in his 2009 book, *Drive: The Surprising Truth About What Motivates Us, [Pin09]* pointing out that today's work mainly comprises creative, complex, "right brain" activities. Pink cites research that shows the best motivators in such an environment are autonomy, mastery, and purpose:

- *Autonomy* provides employees with freedom over some or all of the four main aspects of work: when they do it, how they do it, who they do it with, and what they do.

- *Mastery* encourages employees to become better at a subject or task that matters to them and allows for continuous learning.

- *Purpose* gives people an opportunity to fulfil their natural desire to contribute to a cause greater and more enduring than themselves.

Pink is not the only one to support claims that these motivators are what lead to people performing better. In her research, Margareth J. Wheatley[5] establishes a clear causality between participation and autonomy on one hand and productivity on the other. Her research shows that productivity gains in truly self-managed work environments start at a minimum of 35% higher than in traditionally managed organizations.

> Self-managing working environments are 35% more productive.

With Daniel Pink's book and Margaret J. Wheatley's research in mind, knowing that highly motivated people perform best, and considering our own observations of managerial selection breaking down as a company grows, we started to look more closely at self-selection as a tool to design our teams.

What better place to start offering autonomy than by letting staff members decide for themselves which team they would prefer to work in?

Self-Selection Has a Good (and Interesting) Track Record

Self-selection is neither a new nor an unproven idea. Leo McKinstry described one of the earliest and most successful large-scale self-selections in his 2009 book *Lancaster—The Second World War's Greatest Bomber [McK95]* about the Royal Air Force's Lancaster bomber crews in the early 1940s.

Lancaster crews were tightly knit, and survival and success on a Lancaster depended entirely on the intimate understanding among the crew members. That critically close relationship among airmen underpinned the self-selection process used to form bomber crews.

Recruits were trusted to form their own crews without any guidance from senior commanders. There were no rules and no restrictions, other than the number of airmen and skills needed to man an aircraft. McKinstry explains that the trainees had to rely on gut instinct when selecting a group to join.

Fast-forward to 2004 when Atlassian, an Australian Internet company, created the ShipIt Day concept: a twenty-four-hour hackathon that lets employees choose their own projects and teams to build something unconnected to their regular jobs in a single day.

Originally named "FedEx Day" after FedEx's 1980's slogan, "When it absolutely, positively has to be there overnight," ShipIt Day went on to become highly successful and gained worldwide popularity after it was cited by Daniel Pink in his book *Drive*.

---

5.   http://www.margaretwheatley.com/articles/goodbyecommand.html

Numerous companies around the world including Spotify, Atlassian, Nintendo, and many others organize ShipIt Days on a regular basis to kick-start innovation, focus on the importance of speedy delivery, and simply have fun and learn new things.

In this spirit we had many ShipIt Days at Trade Me, and it was always a joy to see an entire organization self-select into small teams, self-organize, and work on projects of their own choosing. During one memorable day we had roughly eighty people in fifteen teams working on fifteen projects that they had designed to benefit the company in one way or another.

We saw ShipIt Day as a study in what happens when you give a group of people complete freedom to work on what they think is important, with whomever they like, and using whichever approach (agile certainly wasn't prescribed) they think will work best to get the job done.

When employees self-selected into teams for ShipIt Day we observed the following:

- People naturally form *small, cross-functional teams*. Teams are between three and six people and team composition is based on skill rather than role. There is no one person per skill, and those T-shaped people who are good at collaborating are in high demand.

- No one chooses to work on more than *one team or project.* Time and again organizations fall into the trap of optimizing resources rather than focusing on outcomes. People often believe that multitasking, having people work across several projects, and focusing on resource utilization are the keys to success, when in reality they're not. It's interesting to note that when employees are determined to ship, no one thinks it's best to do more than one thing at a time and nobody worries about utilization during a ShipIt Day! And nobody believes they are more valuable as specialists across teams than as generalizing specialists within one team.

- People communicate *face to face.* There are barely any discussions about process or how to communicate. Team members just talk and coordinate and collaborate as needed. Things are much faster that way. This is also most likely why, even though our company spans three cities, all of the teams decided for themselves to be 100% co-located. This meant that even when the "ideal" person wasn't on site, they felt it would be better to go with someone who was in the room and who would work outside their usual boundaries.

- A *shared, clear goal* makes everything so much easier. When people buy into the goal and know clearly the problem they're solving and understand why it's a problem, things become a lot easier for everyone. It's easy to make decisions and reach consensus when everyone understands and supports the objectives and constraints around a project or product. Selecting what they wanted to work on offered great benefits for ensuring that the team had a shared and compelling goal.

- Team members are *highly motivated*, enjoy the experience, and get lots of work done. Some of the projects people built, such as an "Is Someone in the Shower?" application for reducing wait times for people in the office who exercised (no, it didn't involve a camera; it was a light switch sensor), a virtual receptionist, or the room-booking app "Get a Room," were simply incredible additions to the office and are still in use today.

Seeing everyone so happy and motivated before, during, and after ShipIt Day, we couldn't help but wonder whether we could find a way to allow employees to choose who to work with and what to work on in their normal working lives too.

Sandy remembers:

> For us, that ShipIt Day was a real lightbulb moment. We realized that we could take the way in which people organize themselves when they want to achieve something and apply it to the entire organization. That's what we wanted to do: apply those principles to achieve our goal of total squadification.

What Next?

In this chapter we looked at what's behind successful teams. Anyone who has ever been part of a high-performing team will know what it feels like when a group of people truly begin to gel, when everyone is committed to and enthusiastic about a shared goal, and when people know each other well enough to both support and hold each other accountable for great performance. These high-performing teams exist in software development and also in sports or in any area where a group of people need to manage their interdependencies while working toward a shared, compelling goal.

We established two options for structuring your workplace into teams—managerial selection and self-selection—and we introduced guidelines for when each of them is appropriate to use. By now you should be able to suggest self-selection as a valid approach at your organization and explain why it's a good idea.

Next we'll show you how to prepare for a large-scale self-selection event. You will get ideas, tools, and advice including a checklist for assessing your readiness, guidelines for the right number of rules and constraints, advice on logistics, and insights for how to create a custom-made facilitation plan.

CHAPTER 2

Preparing for a Self-Selection Event

In the following two chapters we outline everything you need to know to prepare for a successful self-selection event, from checking that you're ready to getting the materials in place for the event itself. We explain why this level of preparation is important and discuss some of the challenges you can expect along the way.

In this chapter we guide you through the things you need to think about and prepare weeks or months in advance. How much time you need before your self-selection event depends on the scale. As a rule of thumb, if your event involves more than sixty people, you'll need to start planning at least six weeks in advance.

We also guide you through how to conduct a readiness check, get permission to run the event, communicate the concepts and plan, coordinate the logistics, as well as under which circumstances to run a trial event.

Preparation is vital! Before we start on the initial steps, it's important to emphasize how vital it is to prepare well in advance. In fact, we suggest erring on the side of overpreparation, mainly because it will give you the best chance of success, and also because it will put your mind at ease and make you a more relaxed facilitator.

Self-Selection at Scale

The most immediate question we faced at Trade Me was how we could facilitate a self-selection event at scale. Should we follow the Lancaster bombers' lead to get everyone into a giant hall and simply tell them to get on with it? Or was there a more structured way that would make the people involved more comfortable?

We tried researching the concept, but it appeared that either no one had carried out a self-selection event at this scale before or, if they had, they hadn't published the process or results. This meant we had to design and develop our own self-selection process from scratch.

We spent months planning our first squadification and put an incredible amount of thought into the details.

Sandy describes what was involved in those early stages:

> After we had made the decision to run a self-selection event, we spent months planning it. We had to come up with ideas for how to facilitate it, so we ran a trial in one of our satellite businesses. In the end we spent a full day just preparing the office materials we would need—cutting out photos of more than 150 people, making templates, and creating visual signals for ready/non-ready squads.

> We spent a lot of time setting up and creating the environment. Even though we didn't control what was happening during the day, we put a lot of time and effort into creating an environment that would be as conducive as possible to a successful event.

Now that you understand that you're going to have to roll up your sleeves to start planning your event, we'll explain the steps in detail to ensure that you're ready to conduct your own self-selection event. The following graphic shows the first six steps of the process:

PREPARING FOR SELF-SELECTION

Step 1: Conduct a Readiness Check
Step 2: Run a Trial
Step 3: Get Permission
Step 4: Define the Teams to Select
Step 5: Coordinate Logistics
Step 6: Communicate Early and Often

We start with how you can identify whether you're ready to run an event and what you'll need to have in place up front.

Step 1: Conduct a Readiness Check

We believe that any company could run a self-selection event, or at the very least be able to actively demonstrate the principle of giving people autonomy to choose whom they work with. To get started, you'll need to ask yourself a series of questions in order to understand whether you have everything in place to be successful. The following checklist outlines the considerations you should make before you embark on self-selection:

ARE YOU READY FOR SELF-SELECTION CHECKLIST

☐ Do you have, or can you get, support from senior management?

☐ Are people open to trying self-selection?

☐ Is this the right time to self-select?

☐ Do you or can you have stable cross-functional teams?

☐ Do you feel personally ready to try this?

☐ Are you confident that this can work in your organization?

☐ Are you ready to answer people's questions?

☐ Have you considered a trial or a twenty-four-hour hackathon?

If you answer no to any of these questions, that's okay. Don't give up! It just means you might have slightly more groundwork to do. It's important to know your starting point, and we'll talk you through some of the ways to make progress in each of these areas.

In some cases you may need to tackle other problems in the run up. For example, if you're still discussing whether people can work in stable, cross-functional teams, you may struggle to get employees to choose a new home. In that case you may want to dedicate some time to researching, experimenting, and problem solving first. In our case, before embarking on self-selection we certainly had to identify and work through a number of problems, including staff members working on too many projects and having ad hoc project teams formed and disbanded according to whichever project was highest priority at the time. By the time we self-selected, we had tested and demonstrated why small, stable, cross-functional teams were the way forward.

While the previous questions are aimed at the company, it's also important to consider if you yourself are fully prepared. It's likely that people will have lots of questions and probably some criticisms, so it's important you be ready for lots of upcoming conversations and persuasion.

> Only after we had proven the success of working in small, cross-functional teams in one part of the organization did we look into scaling the approach elsewhere.

We would be lying if we told you we weren't nervous about embarking on our first self-selection event. We were acutely aware that we were reorganizing one of New Zealand's most iconic businesses using a process that was unproven at the time. We honestly had no idea whether it was going to work! By the time you finish this book, you should be confident that the process will work and feel reassured by the case study, but you should still be prepared to be challenged and questioned as you suggest something that may be radically different from what your organization has done in the past.

Managers and coworkers are likely to ask you questions and voice concerns; it could be to test your ability to persevere or to discuss genuine concerns about the event itself. The most frequently asked questions before a self-selection event are usually these:

- What if a fight breaks out as people argue over joining one squad?

- What if someone gets picked on and pushed around by others?

- What if one person ends up standing in the corner on his own like the last kid chosen for sports at school?

- What if people want to join a squad they are totally unskilled and inappropriate for?

- What if one particular squad or area is very popular?

- What if no one wants to work in a particular area?

- What if no one turns up, out of fear or because they don't like the idea of self-selection?

The questions you will be asked could be somewhere along those lines, and you should expect to be asked lots of questions. You will know the people involved and how best to handle your responses, but it may also be helpful to refer to responses like these:

- We have an expectation that employees will behave like trusted adults and resolve their problems themselves.

- We have confidence in the process; it has been tested it and it works.

- When we choose teams by managerial selection we often get things wrong.

- It's worth a try.

- Even if it doesn't fully work, we will learn a lot about the staff, their preferences, and their relations, which will be useful for whichever direction we choose to take.

Self-selection can be a scary concept. There's no certainty that self-selection will work for you, but thorough preparation will help reduce the uncertainty as much as possible and increase the likelihood of success.

If you're still debating whether to go ahead at this point, one way to get an insight into the potential outcome is to consider running your own ShipIt Day and ask people to self-select into teams for the day. This will allow you to see how they react to self-selection in a safe environment. If they can figure out how to self-select for a twenty-four-hour hackathon, there's a good chance they'll figure it out in real life, too. It will also make employees feel more confident when you can point to a real and recent example they've been part of. (You can read more about ShipIt Day on page 7.)

Step 2: Run a Trial

After you determine that you and your organization fulfill the prerequisites for self-selection, the next step is to run a trial self-selection event to become familiar with the process and mitigate risks by anticipating and addressing them in a smaller context. A trial in this sense is a scaled-down self-selection with fifteen to twenty people (or two to four teams), which will give you a lot of information at little cost. (If your self-selection involves fewer than thirty people, your life will be easier, and there's no need to run a trial first. You can go directly to Step 4 on page 20.)

We opted to carry out a trial self-selection event at one of our satellite offices, which gave us a more controlled environment and fewer people with whom to test and refine our process. We ran the event with just twenty employees and started with a crudely defined process, which involved iterations, discussions, and lots of sticky notes with names on them. By the end of the day, twenty people had self-selected into three squads, and we knew that we now had a basic process that we could refine to work with any number of people.

All of the employees in the newly selected squads were either in the team they wanted to be in or fully understood the reason why they had chosen differently. The level of buy-in to the outcome was far higher than anything we'd seen before. Had it not worked, we wouldn't have lost too much either—maybe some of our own time—but we still would have learned a lot about the people and the teams involved.

> The level of buy-in was far higher than anything we had seen before.

In order to run a trial, you need only a few things: a group of people you believe are willing to try something new, a list of the teams to form, and photographs of those involved. For a small-scale trial all you need to do is place empty pieces of paper with the squad names on the wall, one for each squad, and hand everyone their photographs, asking them to place their photo in the squad they want to work in. If they don't come up with a good solution during the first iteration of ten minutes, discuss what's missing and try another iteration. If you keep it informal and low key, you'll have the opportunity to learn a lot.

When we ran our initial trial, we formed our first squads in this way, which gave us the opportunity to fine-tune our process for the bigger self-selection event. The main issues highlighted by our trial were these:

- *We needed to speed up the process.* Going into our trial we believed that a full day would be plenty of time, but we almost had to continue the next day. We didn't want this process to take so long, so rather than extend the time frame, we focused on identifying ways to speed up the selection process. We realized that better visual management was key.

- *We needed to make everything bigger, bolder, and brighter so that it would be easy to interpret the status of a squad at a glance.* As you can see in the figure on page 17, our early attempts at visualization were not that great. Big color photographs and green check marks and red Xes would be very helpful to indicate whether a squad is complete.

- *We needed to create momentum and cadence.* We decided to build in specific time slots and focus on moving forward quickly, thus keeping the momentum until the final squads were formed.

- *We needed to provide pre-event communication.* We found this to be incredibly important, perhaps even more important than what we do on the day itself. We had made assumptions for the trial, and in hindsight it would have made sense to explain things in far more detail and make sure that people knew what to expect. For example, one of the things we missed was offering a detailed explanation of the roles of scrum master

and product owner. While focusing on the process of self-selection, we hadn't put enough effort into making sure that people's key questions about these roles were answered.

Of all the things we learned during our trial, one of the most powerful was that many of our original fears were unfounded: there were no fights, no people crying in the corner, and no empty squads at the end of the day.

An alternative trial

An alternative way to try out the process is to run a fake self-selection event, where you can test the concept and refine it without risk. This would involve coworkers picking squads but not having to work in them later, simply following the self-selection process to learn how it works. We've known companies that do this, and it could work well for you too—just be aware that people behave very differently when they're not making real choices. It's like playing poker for no money: players will throw their chips around when they have nothing to lose.

Step 3: Get Permission

Once you've decided that you want to go with self-selecting teams, you'll have to convince others in the organization that it's a good idea. You don't just walk up and say "Hey, we want to do this" and then do it. Many people need to be convinced, and you'll need to manage their expectations.

It's unlikely that you'll get complete buy-in for self-selection from the outset. If you know you can, great. If not, you'll have to start selling your idea and persuading the staff that self-selection is the right way forward.

Initial Buy-In May Be Difficult

Depending on where you are in the management hierarchy, you may find that seeking forgiveness after the fact, rather than asking for permission beforehand, is the best way forward.

The question we're most often asked is, "How did you get management to agree?" We didn't have full buy-in at Trade Me in the beginning, but at least it was an organization that operated on trust where managers were inclined to give you enough rope to try something new.

We felt we needed to just go ahead and do it rather than try to persuade everyone at first. While we didn't ask for permission, we didn't act like cowboys either. We moved slowly and kept everyone in the loop along the way. Our aim was full transparency from start to finish. In fact, we probably erred on the side of over-communicating, but at least we were explaining what was actually going to happen rather than asking whether it would be a good idea.

Sandy remembers what it felt like:

> *We were scared ourselves. We didn't know whether this was going to work. We were waiting for someone to stop us at some point because we were doing something that felt so outside of everyone's comfort zone. We were expecting a tap on the shoulder, someone telling us, "Stop, you can't do this," but it never came. And that was quite scary in itself. We went higher and higher up in management explaining what we were planning to do, and everyone just said, "Yeah, awesome. Do it. But have you thought of these fifty reasons why it's never going to work?"*

We talked a lot about risk and were very honest about the fact that we didn't know for sure whether our idea would work. What we did know, however, was that the worst-case scenario wasn't so bad. Ultimately, the worst thing that could happen was a day of lost productivity, which we were able to put a monetary value on. We explained that if this didn't work, we could easily move back to managerial selection but with a lot more information than before.

Also, there was risk associated with managerial selection, too. There's no certainty that what managers come up with will be a good solution either.

That's what we talked about and recommend you steer the conversation toward, too: the small size of the risk. What's the worst that can happen?

We were also in a position of strength by having already run a trial event, which meant we knew what was to come and could manage expectations accordingly. If you have doubts whether self-selection will work for you at scale, try running a trial.

In your communication to get permission, the key is being transparent, honest, and determined. You will see that you'll get a long way with this!

Stages of Acceptance

We know from experience that people will likely feel scared or challenged by a concept like this in the beginning. Often their first reaction is shock and surprise, and they usually present you with a long list of fears and reasons why self-selection probably won't work. While accompanying coworkers on their journey toward enthusiasm for or at least acceptance of the idea, we discovered that most people, including us, seem to go through a number of stages.

Stage 1: Doubt (What if It Doesn't Work?)

At the very beginning people are taken aback by the idea and voice fears mostly in the form of "what-if" scenarios. We usually hear the following:

- "What if everyone wants to work in this area?"
- "What if no one wants to work in that area?"
- "What if I don't know what I want?"
- "What if I make the wrong choice?"
- "What if it ends up in total chaos?"
- "What if no one wants to work with this person?"

The main sentiment is "Nice idea, but really, this is not going to work." We went through that ourselves and then realized that everyone would go through similar stages. At some point we walked around the business and watched jaws drop when we explained what we were thinking of doing.

During this first stage the most important issue is to take everyone's fears seriously and to acknowledge their concerns. Take the time to talk through their worries and ideas, but slowly encourage them to see the opportunities.

Stage 2: Inspiration (What if It Does Work?)

At this stage people begin to see the potential of self-selection. The power of the idea of working with whomever they want on whatever they want begins to take shape in their consciousness. It's now seen as a far-fetched but feasible option.

It's very important in this stage to keep communicating. We recommend utilizing all company presentations, group meetings, emails, and one-on-ones. (For more information see Step 6: Communicate Early and Often on page 25.)

Stage 3: Acceptance (How Will We Make It Work?)

Employees start to realize that self-selection is a serious option and that issues will be overcome. They start to trust the process and actively support the idea.

During this stage a lot will depend on you being able to make them trust you—trust that you are well prepared, have thought through potential issues, and have a genuine facilitation plan for the day. The best way to achieve this is to be absolutely transparent with everyone involved, including management.

Don't ignore these stages of acceptance. Expect them to happen and be aware of what people will go through. Don't fight or ignore them; anticipate and work with them!

Step 4: Define the Teams to Select

Once you've defined your readiness, gotten permission, and evaluated whether you should run a trial, it's time to define the squads that people will select into. It's possible to give people a roadmap and product strategy to determine which squads are required, but for us this proved to be too complex. Not only did staff members not know where to start, but they also didn't know how best to meet the needs of the organization.

The squads to establish can reflect your current structure or, if you're not yet working in teams, you'll need to make a decision about which squads are needed. For us this was a complex proposition that required company-wide reflection about our mid- to long-term goals and priorities. We wanted to make sure that our squads would have a purpose that went beyond the current project so that we could reap the performance gains that come with stable squads.

At first the company-wide prioritization involved only the executive team and was heavily tied to our strategy. But when the employees heard about the plan to establish stable squads, they understandably wanted to get this right. We kept a strong eye on our company strategy but also established a simple process to submit a request for a new squad: if you wanted a squad that could support a feature stream, a product, or an area of the business, the executives would consider it for inclusion. In the end, the executives simply voted on the squads they wanted to create.

It wasn't easy to establish exactly how many squads we needed, and we knew that the number of people in a squad would vary (between three and seven), but we also knew that gaps could be filled by future hiring, so we focused on business needs and erred on the side of slightly too many squads rather than not enough.

We planned to create a total of twenty-two new squads across three locations (Auckland, Wellington, and Christchurch in New Zealand). Similar to Spotify's structure on page 4 we already had co-located tribes in place in each city. With property and motors being in Auckland, for example, marketplace and dating in Wellington, and jobs in Christchurch, we were never in doubt about in which location we would need to create a squad.

Having prioritized and planned for the squads, we next needed to paint a clear picture of their purpose so that participants could choose what they wanted to work on and the kind of problems they would solve.

For our Squadification Day we wanted each squad to have the following:

- A squad name
- A clear vision and mission for what it would do
- A product owner

We did this because we didn't want anyone walking out of the self-selection event feeling like they weren't sure what they had selected into, or worse, thinking farther down the line that "this is not what I signed up for."

Establish Squad Names and Missions

We prefer squads to have a clear mission rather than to be general purpose. In his 2002 book, *Leading Teams: Setting the Stage for Great Performances* *[Hac02]*, J. Richard Hackman cites research showing how teams need to have a clear, challenging, and consequential purpose to engage members' motivation and to orient them in a common direction. Without purpose, collaboration will suffer and the squad will never reach a high-performing stage.

Defining the purpose of a squad is a task best suited to the product owner. The product owner is, after all, the person in the best position and able to give examples of the kind of things members could work on in a particular squad. This was something of a balancing act because we didn't want to promise certain projects or a specific roadmap that might change and lead team members to question whether they had signed up for something that didn't turn out to be true.

The better the product owners can explain their squad, its mission, and how they themselves work, the better chance they have of attracting a great squad and, just as important, the right squad to match them and their working styles.

Here are examples of the names and missions for some of our squads:

- The Buyer Squad: Make our buyers' lives easier.

- The Fashion Squad: Create an awesome experience for buying and selling clothes.

- The iPad Squad: Create a great user experience on the iPad.

- The Business Operations Squad: Make the lives of our operations and customer service squads nice and easy.

Most of these squads supported a specific group of end users or a platform. We tried to avoid component squads because we strongly believed that having an end-to-end view and a customer-centric purpose would give us the best results.

We're also strong advocates of allowing squads to choose their own name. The names we initially chose for self-selection were preliminary names to reflect the purpose, but we had no issue with squads changing their names after they had kicked off. Even if that decision was to keep the suggested name, it was important that they had the decision in their own hands, thus hopefully creating a greater sense of ownership.

Preselect Certain Roles

The Lancaster bomber squads described in Self-Selection Has a Good (and Interesting) Track Record on page 7 self-selected with an engineer and second gunner already in place. The engineer needed to undergo specialized training, and the second gunner would join at a later stage. The pilot, bomb aimer, first gunner, wireless operator, and navigator then self-selected into squads with those two roles preassigned.

Since our product owners were quite specialized, often with years of industry experience in one area of the business, we opted for preselecting the product owner for each squad. We deemed it too risky to encourage, for example, a product owner with years of experience in trading cars to move to one of our real-estate squads.

Another reason we chose to preselect the product owners is that they're the people who give the squads direction. This turned out to be beneficial because it meant that we had a relevant and competent person to explain about the squad at the event itself.

Andy Kelk, technology lead for digital mailbox at Australian Post, made a different choice, where he chose to pair a product owner with a scrum master before letting the teams self-select:

> I think what was a really big benefit was having those iteration managers (scrum masters) and product owners tied up from the start and having them as the real kernel of the team. Giving that team an identity was really, really important. We actually spent quite a bit of time trying to pair up those iteration managers and product owners. That in itself was a whole exercise, which required a lot of bravery from those people because they had to put themselves out there and choose each other and do a bit of a "speed date." That was a fairly confronting experience for them, but it really cemented those relationships, which meant that those teams had a kernel.

It's entirely up to you which roles, if any, you choose to preassign. We recommend to choose as few as possible to honor the spirit of self-selection.

Decide if You Will Start from Scratch

It's also important to decide whether your self-selection event will be starting from scratch (empty squads) or if you already have some people who will have to work in a specific area, perhaps for experience reasons or a rare specialist skill. If you do have preselected people, it's important to reflect this openly, because otherwise any done deals would make employees see the process as rigged and put your event at risk.

The advantages of starting completely from scratch are that it can be simpler and easier to throw out any current constraints and starting from a blank sheet can be easier for everyone. It can reduce the complexity of the problem and allow people to consider options they may not have otherwise realized would be possible.

On the other hand, starting from the status quo—reflecting a current team structure as the starting point—makes the process real, and it helps those who want to stay exactly where they are to do so and not feel like they're being bumped.

Step 5: Coordinate Logistics

Establishing early where and when your self-selection event will take place can support your communication effort, build trust that it will actually happen, and give confidence to people that everything is planned and under control.

You should define the following details as early as possible. When will your event take place? Where it will take place? Who will be there?

When Will Your Event Take Place?

It's a good idea to choose a date that's far enough in the future to give people time to get used to the idea but not so far out that it doesn't feel real or could be in danger of not happening at all. Consider also having a backup date in case of last-minute problems or illness of key people.

In a sufficiently large company there will always be people who are ill, traveling, on annual leave, or unable to attend for some other reason whichever date you choose. Therefore, we recommend identifying key personnel up front—those people who without them the event would be compromised.

Following our first self-selection event, Sandy remembers:

> If you have close to 150 participants, it's inevitable that some are going to be away. We didn't look out for our key people being away, and what happened to us was that one of the key influential people was not present on the day. This shouldn't have been a problem per se, but his peers started second-guessing him and they started acting and thinking, "What do you think Peter would want us to do?" rather than choosing for themselves what they wanted to do. It's something we actually had to intervene with during the day because people were slipping away from the principles of self-selection.

Where Will Your Event Take Place?

You'll need a big, open collaborative area with lots of wall space to visualize the status of your squads and the progress of the self-selection process. The event room space we used is shown in the image on page 25.

We had lots of room and lots to discuss! Go for the biggest space you can find and, if possible, run the event away from your normal office environment. This will help detach people from their current project and way of working.

Who Will Be Invited?

It's important to define up front who should take part in your self-selection event. Is there any particular group who should be included or excluded? It's

likely that most people to invite will be obvious, but others will be borderline between being part of a squad or in the supporting cast. In our case we had to make choices about operations, infrastructure, and data analytics specialists.

We recommend that you allow as many employees to self-select as possible. If in doubt, include everyone who could be included in a squad. This should give the best results for your organization and the most diverse squads. It will send an important signal of trust and transparency to everyone.

We advise against inviting those who aren't directly involved in squad work or helping as facilitators. People often act differently when observers or their managers are present.

Step 6: Communicate Early and Often

Communicating fully and correctly might be the single most important thing you can do to give your self-selection the best possible chance of success.

Self-selection is a new and seemingly risky process to many people, and while their first reaction can be quite positive, they can move quickly to fear and resistance: fear of something new and different, fear of what might happen, fear of being stuck with someone they don't get along with, or fear of being stuck in a squad that they can't change their mind about later. Fear and uncertainty aren't something most people want to deal with in their workplace, and your communication needs to allay those fears and clear up any uncertainty.

In our example, the participants had a lot of questions, understandably so because not only were we asking them to choose who they wanted to work with on a daily basis, but we were also asking them in essence who they wanted their new work family to be! By engaging with our coworkers early we surfaced these questions before the event, and we were able to individually answer them and follow up.

In fact, we were actually bombarded with emails, meeting invites, and questions from all angles after we started communicating about squadification. In the early stages we fielded a lot of what-if questions. What if someone gets picked on during the event? What if no one wants to join one particular squad or work with one particular developer? (Every company has one and we were no different.)

We were fairly confident from our trial that these things wouldn't happen at all, but regardless, we were also able to answer that we would be carefully facilitating the session, so no bullying would be allowed. For example, if no one wanted to join one of our squads, this would actually be incredibly useful information that would feed into any future prioritization and tell us that we were probably trying to establish a squad that shouldn't be established.

We recommend the following steps in your approach to communication:

- Talk to as many people as possible, right through the process.

- Actively listen to their concerns and acknowledge and record them.

- Be patient with participants as they work through their fears.

- Record any concerns and the what-if scenarios so that they can be addressed.

- Paint a very honest picture about the worst-case scenario, which is never as bad as people think.

- Talk to staff members individually and present to groups.

- Be clear about why you're doing this and emphasize that you're placing trust in employees to solve the problem.

For our biggest self-selection event we started talking to managers first, in particular with those we knew shared our confidence that employees could be trusted to solve a complex puzzle. That allowed us to speak next to the ones who suggested that self-selection would never work, but by then we had already gathered wider support.

From the supporters we were able to confirm the process and details. For the dissenters we could have robust discussions to iron out any fears, assumptions, or requests.

With the first batch of folks on our side, we started actively communicating with the wider organization and likely participants. Here's the very first email we sent to everyone several weeks before the squadification event:

> Hey Tech,
>
> This email is about moving to squads faster than we have done so far. To date we have seen solid progress in our move to our new squad format and we now have six established squads. The current squad rollout has been purposely slow and controlled. That has been fine so far but we have asked ourselves the question recently, how can we move faster to where we want to be?
>
> We'll be sending out further information to those people directly involved closer to the time and for now just watch this space!
>
> David & Sandy

We soon followed up with a more detailed email where we explained that squadification would be done by self-selection and why we had chosen to do so. We reminded everyone about their successful self-selection on ShipIt Day and that we believed that every day should be like ShipIt Day.

We were, of course, not advocating for twenty-four-hour sprints but believed that the best results would come about if people could choose what to work on and who to work with. We also let everyone know that it would be a facilitated process where we would make sure that nothing got out of hand.

Next we presented to the whole company on the principles of self-selection. We outlined the problems we were aiming to solve, what the intended approach was, and why we thought self-selection was the best option. We gave the staff as much information as we could to make sure everyone knew what to expect at the event.

We really tried to make this presentation as inspiring as we could because we wanted to make sure the employees were aware how much of a privilege it was to be trusted with the company's structure. We made sure to express our confidence in their ability to come up with a great solution—after all, they had already proved they could during ShipIt Day.

The last two weeks before the event we spent answering questions and discussing people's hopes and fears.

Sandy remembers:

> It felt like we were running a PR campaign. In fact, we probably were running a PR campaign: emails, all-company meetings, one-on-one meetings, and conversations at lunch and on the way to the bathroom (even in the bathroom!). We put strong focus on conveying this in these conversations: "We don't think we have the answers. We think you do. We can provide the environment and the facilitation techniques but we're asking you to solve the puzzle." Ultimately, just saying to people "Look, we trust you to do this" seemed to be the tipping point.

What Next?

Now that you've learned how to move the big pieces into place, such as conducting a readiness check, getting permission, and communicating the concepts and plan, you're ready to move on to the next phase: preparing for the day of the event.

CHAPTER 3

Getting Ready for the Day

It's now time to focus on the details of the final preparation for the self-selection event. With only days to go before the big day, you need to decide on the rules and constraints, devise a good facilitation plan, write your FAQs, and organize your materials and stationery. At the end of this chapter you will be ready to go! Here's what's left to do:

```
PREPARING FOR SELF-SELECTION (CONT.)

  Step 1: Define the Rules and Constraints
  Step 2: Create a Facilitation Plan
  Step 3: Prepare FAQs
  Step 4: Prepare Materials and Stationery
```

Step 1: Define the Rules and Constraints

Like anything in life, self-selection comes with a few rules and constraints, although we recommend keeping the number of these to an absolute minimum. Keeping the rules short and simple makes the problem of establishing new squads and choosing the right people easier to solve. We believe that the more rules there are, the more complex the puzzle.

The essence of the process is that you are entrusting people to solve a problem, which is why you need to make sure that they have the freedom to do so within sensible boundaries.

Establish the Main Rules

We have only ever had three rules for our self-selection events:

1. Squads have to be capable of delivering end to end.

2.   Squads have to be made up of three to seven people.

3.   Squads have to be co-located.

Here's the reasoning behind our rules:

Keep Squads Autonomous

Squads have to be capable of delivering end to end.

You don't want to create a web of interdependencies. Squads are given autonomy, and you can't have autonomy unless people have the ability to work on their own. This means squads must have all the skills to work end to end. To become a self-sufficient unit they can't be relying on anyone outside the squad. This doesn't mean that they need the best people; it simply means that they need people with all the skills or the ability to learn these skills to move from an idea to a shipped product or feature.

Keep Squads Small

Squads have to be made up of three to seven members.

Experience has shown us that smaller squads work best. While smaller is usually better, two people is a pair and not really a team—so the minimum number is three. We've also experienced that teams larger than ten become unwieldy and unproductive, and they often form subgroups that can introduce conflict.

Agile experts often assert that teams should be made up of seven plus/minus two people;[1] however, we prefer even smaller teams where possible. This encourages cross-functional collaboration and supports the concept of members wearing different hats rather than only performing tasks within their respective professional fields. (Examples include testers doing business analysis and developers volunteering to test.) Small teams also make communication easier because there are fewer communication paths among all members—the number of communication paths increases significantly as the number of people increases.

There is an equation to calculate this:[2]

$$paths(n) = \frac{n(n-1)}{2}$$

The number of communication paths per team member is shown in the following chart.

---

1.   http://www.infoq.com/news/2009/04/agile-optimal-team-size
2.   http://mathforum.org/library/drmath/view/61212.html

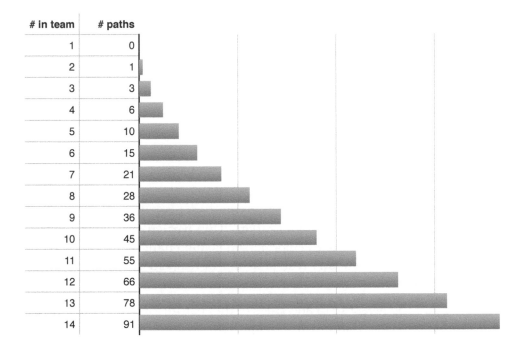

# in team	# paths
1	0
2	1
3	3
4	6
5	10
6	15
7	21
8	28
9	36
10	45
11	55
12	66
13	78
14	91

We recommend you set the number of people as a clear constraint and to allow the squads to work out how they will manage within that constraint. In our case, if they asked questions such as "Can we have half a person?" our answer was "Absolutely, if you think that this is the best available option and fits the constraint." As it turned out, those who suggested half a person later always withdrew that suggestion when they considered how this would work in reality.

Keep Squads Together

Squads have to be co-located.

If you can, keep your squads co-located. Co-location is one of the most important features of the highest performing software development teams. While it might be possible to create squads across locations, it will make communication and collaboration so much harder. Sometimes distributed teams can't be avoided, but if you can work from the same room, we recommend you do so!

Don't Specify the Outcome Before You Start

We've usually been asked and always resisted requests to specify up front the number of senior and/or junior members for each squad. The intention of the request can be to ensure that the right amount of technical know-how is present and that there is an even distribution of the most experienced people across squads. However, this request assumes that preselecting based on those features would be more successful than choosing on the day. To us this feels uncomfortably like management selection.

If you did choose to take this additional rule on board and specify, for example, one senior developer for every squad, you could easily find out on the day that you don't have the right ratio of talent in your organization. This particular request also assumes that one senior person is interchange-

> Remember, these are people, not plug compatible "resources."

able with another, which isn't true of senior developers any more than it is of any other role.

Not bowing to the pressure to add rules of this nature also prevents a highly undesirable outcome, that in which employees perceive that they've actually been selected into predefined allocations and it wasn't self-selection at all. It's our belief that the only thing worse than management selection is a fake version of self-selection where people are led to believe they will self-select only to find out the decision wasn't theirs at all, and due to the rules and constraints, their new position was effectively preselected.

> ### Key principle: Do what is best for your company
>
> Our overarching principle, as opposed to an additional rule, was "Do what is best for your company." It proved incredibly important to have this principle, especially when problems or stalemates were encountered during the selection process. We displayed this prominently as a large banner at the front of the room, forming a constant reminder that we could refer to at any time during the self-selection process.

Step 2: Create a Facilitation Plan

By now you should have a better idea of how the day might pan out. It's time to ensure that you have a solid facilitation plan in place well before your self-selection event. People can react strangely to new levels of autonomy, and while we've never tried locking them into a room and hoping they sort it out, we're confident it would unlikely be a great outcome or experience for anyone.

As the facilitator it's your job to provide the structure and boundaries for the event, and we highly recommend having a detailed agenda for the day, potentially with contingency plans listed or attached.

David describes how we came up with our first facilitation plan:

> I remember standing in the Wellington office overlooking the waterfront with a blank piece of paper. Each of us had a Sharpie and someone said, "Well, we seem to have permission to do this now, or at least nobody is stopping us. What are we actually going to do?" We looked at each other and I said, "Um, I don't really know."

> Originally we considered whether coworkers would email us their top three choices for squads they wanted to join well in advance. If we ranked them, we could simply assign points to them and assign people to squads in that way. But then we thought, is that actually self-selection, or are we just dressing up management selection differently and with more information? And wouldn't people's requests change when they saw what others had done or new opportunities opened up? We needed everyone to be directly involved in the process. After all, this really was all about them.

> So, we started scribbling things down and tried to come up with some kind of supporting structure and process that would allow us to do this. We knew it would have to involve employees being present and physically making a choice while standing in a room with everyone else as the choices and opportunities developed. This would not be just be another meeting!

From the very first squadification event the basic running order hasn't changed and usually follows these steps:

1. Welcome the participants and kick off the event.

2. Allow the product owners to pitch for their squads.

3. Facilitate several rounds of self-selection, usually three to four time frames of ten minutes, followed by a period to pause and reflect.

4. Wrap up, close the event, and clarify what will happen next.

Over time we've refined our facilitation techniques to guide groups through an iterative approach to self-selection and have incorporated learnings from our own experiences and those of others. The basic process and principles, however, haven't changed since our very first Squadification Day. The process of working through a facilitation plan will cement a lot of the ideas in your head and help you identify any gaps that you should address.

Step 3: Prepare Frequently Asked Questions

Even after lots of conversations, emails, and presentations on the day, it's important to remind everyone of the details of the event, the reasoning behind it, and what to expect.

We recommend collecting the most frequently asked questions and preparing a simple yet comprehensive FAQ sheet for the event. It's a good way to make the details front of mind for participants.

Sample FAQs

Here are sample FAQs you can use or adapt for your self-selection event:

Do I have to stay where I am?

This really *is* self-selection. You don't have to stay where you are if you don't want to—although it's totally fine if you do! You choose!

What squads can I choose from again?

Have a look at the list of all squads and think about things like these:

- What do I want to learn?
- Where would I learn the most?
- Where would I teach the most?
- What is best for the company?

When will I start with my new squad?

It's important to know that this reorganization won't be in place straight away; people have projects to hand over and things to finish. We'll sit with each squad and talk through questions, issues, and current projects, then agree a plan. Hopefully the transition occurs sooner rather than later, but the timing is dependent on who chooses which team.

Can I be in more than one squad?

Our experience tells us that one squad per person is best. It allows people to commit to their teammates and to the work, which means they are always available to their squad. There are exceptions to this, of course, and the decision is ultimately yours.

What should I do if I can't be there on the day?

We would love for everyone to be there, but with this number of people it's inevitable that some won't be able to make it. If you can't be there, don't worry; you can either nominate a proxy (that is, someone you trust who you can explain what you would like to do) or you can let one of the facilitators know.

What about my current work/projects?

This is important and we'll account for this, but don't worry about it right now. We're defining the end goal with self-selection. Once we know the squad layout we'll tackle your current workload.

How many test/design/development slots are there in each squad?

We have a squad blueprint that you will have seen, but this is a suggestion and *not* a strict layout. The exact requirements will vary based on the work (for example, we think operations squads should have a 1:1 test:dev ratio, but it's really up to the squad to decide). If in doubt, talk to the others in a squad and the product owners.

The exact requirements for each squad will vary based on the work; for example, we found that BAU squads work well with a 1:1 test:dev ratio, but it's really up to the squad to decide. Also, some squads might have no design requirements, for example, whereas others will be doing significant front-end work. If in doubt, talk to the others in a squad and the product owners.

I just want someone to tell me where to go. Can you just put me in a squad?

We think *you* know more about what you should work on and whom you should work with. If you're really unsure, you can select the "I have no squad" section initially and then listen for issues and gaps to fill. We really don't want to select on your behalf; you will do a better job!

How long will I be with my squad? Am I signing my life away?

We want stable squads, but you aren't signing your life away. We'll review the lay of the land within six months.

Where should I put my photo if I just don't know where to go?

Just choose the "I have No Squad" section (for now!).

What if someone else is already doing what I want to do?

If someone is already doing what you want to do, talk to that person and the rest of the squad, and do this against a backdrop of finding the best solution for the company.

What happens next?

We will arrange to sit down with each squad to answer any questions and discuss any issues and define a plan for becoming a new squad. That plan will involve a day when the squad sits down as a group and decides which elements of agile will best suit their work (choosing from a list of ingredients). We aren't the scrum police and we don't enforce agile, but we can provide a list of things and help you pick.

Step 4: Prepare Materials and Stationery

Self-selection needs to be an interactive and visual event where everyone can see what's going on and actively participate throughout the process. Following is a checklist of the suggested materials you should have on the day of the event:

MATERIALS YOU WILL NEED

- ☐ Squad diagrams for the wall
- ☐ Photographs of the participants
- ☐ Skills checklists
- ☐ A list of rules and constraints
- ☐ "Do what is best for your company" banner
- ☐ Descriptions of key roles
- ☐ Colored sticky notes to show skill sets
- ☐ A big timer
- ☐ Printouts of your FAQs
- ☐ Squad mission/purpose statements

Empty Squad Diagrams

You'll need an empty squad diagram for each of the squads you want to create. As part of your planning for Step 4 in chapter 2 on page 20 you will have defined the desired squads, and now it's simply a case of creating the sheets so they can be stuck to the wall when employees turn up for your event.

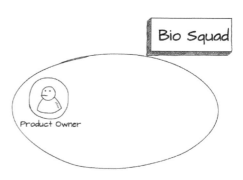

The idea behind this is to have partic-ipants self-select by adding their photos to squad diagrams on the wall. That way you can build a live picture as the self-selection process progresses.

The image shows the layout of an empty squad diagram.

As you can see, the squad sheets were simply circles (or ovals) drawn on poster-sized paper. As simple as this looks, a fair amount of thought had gone into the layout. For example, the circle itself fits a maximum of seven photographs, which corresponds to the constraint that squads should be no more than seven people. There's also a prominent title at the top of the sheet to enable everyone to see each squad at one glance—something we had noticed was important during our trials and is even more important the more squads being selected in one event.

The product owner's picture is positioned on the side and not at the top. This was done on purpose to ensure we didn't inadvertently imply a hierarchy within the squad. The product owner is simply the person with the business knowledge on the squad and not the leader. That person's picture was also taped onto the sheet to make it permanent because the product owner had been preselected and was unlikely to change.

> Preselection doesn't imply hierarchy.

It's also a good idea to prepare a separate squad sheet with the title "Not in a Squad." This is for those who don't know where to go initially. They can put their photos there to demonstrate to others that they are available for selection. This mitigates the risk of anyone hiding in the corner and being missed or inadvertently bypassing the process.

Photographs of Participants

Provide a photo of everyone involved in the self-selection event. Ideally, the photos should be easily recognizable from a distance and the right size for your squad sheets. We had learned from our trial that things go much more quickly when you can easily see the status of each squad and who's in it.

Be aware that preparing these photos can take some time if your event involves a lot of people. With 150 participants, we spent hours printing and cutting out photos from the employee directory (as shown in the photo on page 38) and we really believe that level of effort and organization paid off. It also meant that we systematically went through the plan for the next day in detail and allowed us to pick up on anything we may have missed.

Also, be sure that no participant's photo is missed. Forgetting a few photographs may seem trivial, but it can make the person whose photo is missing feel neglected and unimportant.

Skills Stickers

Skills stickers provide an easy way for people to discuss whether their squad has all the necessary skills and has a status of "ready." In order to facilitate this conversation, provide color-coded sticky notes for people to indicate their skills. The intention is that they can put the sticky notes on top of their photo to display which skills they can cover for a squad.

For our event blue was development, yellow was test, dark pink represented business analysis, light pink designated UX/design, and database skill was gray. You can see an example of the skills stickers we used in the figure on page 39.

Don't be hung up on the actual colors—they're just a quick visual cue about each person's skill(s) and are useful to surface shortages and surpluses. Because each squad will have different skill needs depending on its purpose and technology, it's important to emphasize that the stickies visualize skills, not roles. It's also important to encourage people to use more than one sticky for their photo if they can contribute more than one skill.

Skills Checklists

At the bottom of each squad sheet there are several rip-off sheets for the squad's aggregated skills coverage. Their purpose is to give each squad the opportunity to collectively check off the skills, indicating and visually display-ing whether or not they are complete. Without this, it can be difficult to

quickly assess a squad when people are moving in and out during the self-selection event. Here's a sample skills checklist that goes at the bottom of the squad sheets:

SAMPLE SKILLS CHECKLIST

Product Owner	Squad Master	Dev	Test	Business Analysis	Design UX	Data-base

For each skill, the squad uses a check mark (skill is covered), an X (skill is not adequately covered), or N/A (not applicable, that is, not needed for this squad) to designate its current status. Needs differ for each squad, and not all squads need all skills (for example, an infrastructure squad probably won't need any design skill).

Make sure you have enough of these little strips to use a fresh one for each squad and change it after each self-selection round. We recommend printing enough for four to five rounds per squad.

List of Constraints

Print several copies of your constraints (see our example constraints in the figure that follows) to display around the room. They will be a healthy reminder of the boundaries during the event.

A FULLY FORMED SQUAD IS...

- ☐ Capable of delivering end to end
- ☐ Seven people (+/- two) - think skills not roles
- ☐ Co-located

Role Posters

If you're introducing new roles as part of your self-selection event, it's a good idea to create role description posters in addition to all the other communication you do about these roles. Bring your posters to the self-selection event so that people can have a quick refresher. In our case we found it especially useful to have the role of the squad masters visibly displayed on the walls because participants needed to be clear about the expectations if they were to put up their hand to take on the role in a squad.

Following are the role posters from our self-selection event, which are still on display around the office today.

First is the poster for the squad master role (which is similar to a scrum master but edited for anyone who may choose not to use scrum):

Squad Master

Guide the squad to be magic

- ☐ Makes sure the squad is running an awesome agile development process
- ☐ Assists squad members in adopting and using agile
- ☐ Helps the squad work in the best possible way
- ☐ Protects the squad from disturbance and external threats
- ☐ Is not a project manager but a servant leader with no formal authority

Here is the role poster for the product owner role, which may be new to people who haven't worked on an agile team before:

Product Owner

Build the right thing

- [ ] Ensures the team builds the right product
- [ ] Makes sure business benefits are delivered
- [ ] Prioritizes features and adjusts scope
- [ ] Provides boundaries to describe the realities within which the vision must be realized (for example, time frames, quality)
- [ ] Makes sure stakeholders are informed and the vision is aligned with their wishes

The day before each self-selection event we spend time ensuring we have all the materials we need. This can be quite fun as we cut out photographs of everyone involved, prepare the color coding and checklists, and prepare large squad diagrams prepopulated with any information we already have such as squad names and product owner photos.

What Next?

We've now shown you everything you'll need to do in preparation for your self-selection event. You're ready to go!

You may have slightly different skill requirements or constraints for your squads, and it's up to you to finalize the details. Running through this level of preparation will put your mind at ease, knowing that you'll walk into your self-selection event fully prepared and ready for almost any scenario that might arise.

Next we move on to the event itself, looking at the iterative process in more detail and talking you through the timing and facilitation needed on the big day.

CHAPTER 4

Running a Self-Selection Event

You've put in the work, you've done the preparation—now you're ready to go! In this chapter we show you the steps to make your self-selection a fast-paced and successful event. The detailed step-by-step guide and facilitation plan contain everything you need to know about creating a collaborative environment, setting the context, and running successive self-selection iterations. By the end of this chapter you'll be in a perfect position to turn the outcomes of your self-selection into reality. The following graphic shows the steps to get there:

RUNNING YOUR SELF-SELECTION EVENT

Step 1: Set up the room
Step 2: Welcome people as they arrive
Step 3: Introduce the day
Step 4: Let product owners pitch
Step 5: Explain the rules
Step 6: Get people started: One, two, three, go!
Step 7: Conduct a checkpoint review
Step 8: Rinse and repeat
Step 9: Tackle the outstanding problems
Step 10: Wrap up

Step 1: Set Up the Room

We recommend getting to your venue early so that you have plenty of time to set up the room. You'll need to have all your stationery, photographs, and materials set out in the right places. Make sure to look at the checklist for what to bring on page 36. Before the participants arrive, make sure the items in this checklist are set up and ready to go.

SET UP THE ROOM

- ☐ Squad diagrams
- ☐ Photo table
- ☐ Countdown clock
- ☐ Supporting materials

Squad Diagrams

Hang your empty squad diagrams on the walls. As described in Empty Squad Diagrams on page 36, squad diagrams are the empty placeholders for each of the squads you want to create. Make sure that the squad diagrams are far enough from each other so that people have to physically move to add their photo and join a squad. This will energize everyone and make it easy to see who has chosen which squad just by looking at where they stand during the event.

If you have tribes or business units, the diagrams for the squads within them should be placed next to each other. Not only will this make it easier to see the big picture, but it will also be helpful in the hopefully rare case when a person has to be shared between squads.

The larger your group, the more consideration you'll need to give to placing your squad diagrams. And don't forget to have a "Not in a Squad" diagram as described on page 37. This is useful if people want to highlight that they are available for selection and want to be approached.

Photo Table

Lay out everyone's photograph on a table as shown here so that participants can pick theirs up as they walk in. This is an important step in making everyone feel welcome. It also ensures that people actively take part in the event by moving their photos around. It's also a good idea to place a stack of printed FAQ sheets next to the table. See the Sample FAQs on page 34 for an example.

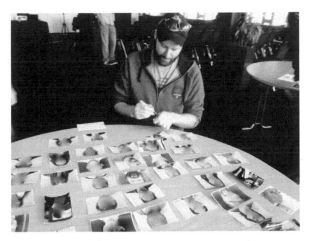

Also important: make sure to double-check that you have everyone's picture. If you forget someone, that person will probably feel excluded, and you'll be off to a bad start. It can happen easily if you have a large group of people, so make sure to cross check the photos with your attendee list.

Countdown Clock

Project a large countdown clock or timer onto the wall so that people can see during the day how far they are into any of the self-selection iterations. A big timer sets the expectation that things will flow and generates a sense of urgency.

If you're unsure whether people will notice that a round has ended, bring a whistle or another instrument that makes a loud noise to signal the end of a round.

Supporting Materials

Display supporting materials on the walls. During the squadification event at Trade Me, we posted explanations of roles that not everyone necessarily understood yet, such as squad master on page 40 and product owner on page 41. We also displayed role posters in several places around the room so that they could feed into any relevant conversations throughout the day.

Another good visual is to prominently display a banner with the words "Do what is best for your company," like the one mentioned on page 32. This can provide a good backdrop for the event and remind participants of the overarching principle of the day.

Here's an example layout of a squadification room:

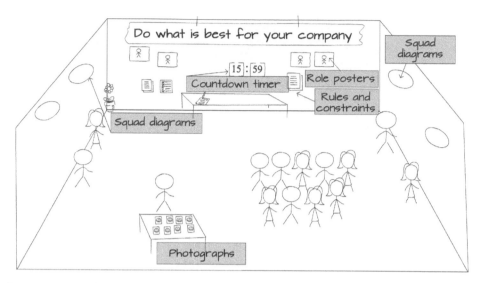

Step 2: Welcome People as They Arrive

Welcome participants as they arrive. Ask them to grab a FAQ sheet (as described on page 34) and their photo and to write their name on their photo. Especially in larger groups or in a fast-growing environment, names are important, because not everyone might know everyone else.

If you have some existing squads, ask the members to put their photo into the corresponding squad diagram on the wall to visualize the status quo. If you don't have any existing squads, ask everyone to hold onto their photo for the upcoming self-selection iterations.

This first interaction of finding their photo, writing their name on it, and, if appropriate, placing it in a squad area is important because it actively involves everyone in the process from the very first moment. And that's exactly what you want—engaged people who own the process and outcomes of self-selection.

Check that the right people are present

Before you kick off the event by introducing the plan for the day, check that the right people are in the room. Is anyone missing? Is anyone present who shouldn't be?

An event like this can act as a magnet for people who don't participate but are interested in the result or simply like to observe. We advise you to politely ask anyone to leave who isn't directly involved in your squadification, either as a squad member or facilitator. This is important because people will often act differently in the presence of those who appear to have power and influence. Check out Who Will Be Invited? on page 24 for who to invite.

Step 3: Introduce the Day

This is the part when you step in front of the group and set the context for the day. Get ready to reiterate the purpose and desired outcomes and to introduce the agenda.

Here's what you need to cover:

- Thank everyone for their time and openness of mind to attend the event.

- Re-emphasize the purpose of the day: to form a number of squads that are capable of delivering solutions to their customers.

- Reiterate why you believe that self-selection is the best way to squadify. Explain why you and your company's management have chosen self-selection. Express your confidence in their ability to come up with the best solution to a complex puzzle. If you're not sure what to say, reread The Science Behind Team Design on page 4.

- Go through the agenda for the day. Explain the outline, including timing.

- Remind participants of the answers to the most commonly asked questions, such as how to deal with those who aren't here or whether people are signing up for life. Talk about anything from the FAQs that's worth mentioning explicitly.

- Let everyone know your expectations. If your self-selection is more than fifty people, it's unlikely that all of the desired squads will be fully formed. Let the group know what success looks like by describing acceptable, desirable, and ideal outcomes.

- Explain what will happen if self-selection doesn't bring about the desired results. Will you go back to managerial selection or try another approach?

- Ask if anyone has any questions. Answer them if they do.

- Express trust and confidence.

- Tell everyone to get ready for the next item on the agenda: the product owner pitches.

The following graphic is a sample agenda for an event with seventy to one hundred people. If you have more or fewer participants, you should adapt your times accordingly.

SELF-SELECTION TIMINGS (SAMPLE)	
1. Set up the room	30-60 mins
2. Welcome	5 mins
3. Introduce the day	10 mins
4. Product owner pitches	30-45 mins
Break	
5. Self-selection round 1	15 mins
6. Self-selection round 2	15 mins
7. Self-selection round 3	15 mins
Break	
8. More self-selection rounds	30-60 mins
9. Define next steps	5 mins
10. Questions then close	5 mins

Step 4: Let Product Owners Pitch

The participants of your self-selection event need to know what they will be signing up for. They need answers to questions such as these:

- What type of work will the squad be doing?

- What is the squad's purpose and mission?

- Who are the customers?

- What will the technical focus be?

It's important for people to make an informed decision and to have the opportunity to help the company solve customer problems in the area they're most passionate about. The best person to introduce a squad's purpose and direction is the product owner.

The product owner owns the product on behalf of the customer. According to the Scrum Primer,[1] the product owner is responsible for maximizing return

> The product owner is the person with business skills on the squad.

on investment by identifying product features, translating these into a prioritized list, and continually reprioritizing and refining the list. The product owner makes sure the squad builds the right thing. You could also say that the product owner is the person with the business skills on the squad. (You can see a list of product owner tasks on page 41.)

Self-selection provides an increased focus on personal relationships, and the future relationship with the product owner is an important consideration. It's important for squad members to hear the pitch "from the horse's mouth" and to have the opportunity to ask questions. The following image shows one of our product owners delivering his pitch.

A good product owner pitch should explain the purpose of the squad and the type of things members will work on. For example:

> *We are going to be the "Seller Squad." Our focus will be to make the sales process on our site easy and delightful. We will take care of anything our sellers want, and we will be driven by the wishes of our five major accounts. The work will be pretty, front-end design stuff with a fast turnaround time.*

If there are current projects, these should be explained too. Remember to make members aware that projects will finish and that choosing a squad is a longer-term commitment beyond the scope of just the current project.

---

1.   http://scrumprimer.org

Those who are new to the organization may find it hard to remember the details of the pitches. If you have a lot of new people, as it is often the case in a rapidly growing organization, provide a printed version of the product owner presentations.

Step 5: Explain the Rules

You're almost ready to go. Now you need to explain the rules and detailed instructions for the self-selection iterations. Start by reiterating what you're looking for in a squad and remind everyone of the constraints for forming squads.

As mentioned in Establish the Main Rules on page 29, the fewer constraints the better. The following have proven successful:

1. Squads have to be capable of delivering end to end.

2. Squads have to be made up of three to seven people.

3. Squads have to be co-located.

Point to the prominently displayed printouts on the wall. Then explain the room layout including the squad diagrams, timer, role posters, and company banner. Next, guide participants through the instructions:

- The iterations will be ten minutes in duration.

- When you hear the word "Go!" place your photo in the squad you'd like to work in.

- Discuss with the other people in your chosen squad whether the squad has the right skills and is fully formed; that is, work within the constraints.

- If the squad doesn't have the right skills or otherwise isn't fully formed, have a conversation with people from other squads and see if you can solve the problem together.

- Allow the last minute or so to fill in the skills checklist (as shown on page 38).

- After each iteration there will be real-time feedback to the room.

Explain that you will run as many iterations as needed to achieve a good result. Ask if anyone has any questions, and if so, answer them. Once everyone understands what they're expected to do, it's time to get started!

Step 6: Get people started: One, Two, Three, Go!

Once you're ready, start the big, visible wall timer to count down from ten minutes. Set off the first self-selection round by shouting "Go!" or blowing your whistle.

On your "Go!" people should start walking around talking to product owners and each other while thinking about which squad they want to join. To choose a squad they stick their photo into the corresponding squad diagram.

As facilitators, our greatest fear was that we'd shout "Go!" and nobody would move. David describes his experience:

> That was my real point of worry: what would happen next. And what happened was that people at first moved really slowly. But they moved. At first, they just hovered by a squad and chatted to someone next to them. They weren't doing anything at this point. They were just watching each other. There were all these empty squad diagrams on the wall, and when someone would take his picture and make a move, everyone would look up thinking, "Where's he going? What's that guy doing?"
>
> Once people started to understand the process, they started talking to each other. "I'm thinking about moving to this squad. What do you think?" People were sharing their thoughts and ideas with each other. It was really great to see. It was slow at first, yes, but then they really got on with it.

We recommend each iteration last for no more than ten minutes. This is enough time for participants to have the conversations they need and to overcome any nerves about moving or selecting a squad. In addition, an efficient time slot is important to keep things moving and to make sure everyone stays focused.

At first, ten minutes may seem like not enough time, but this imposed constraint means people will be motivated to make decisions within the allotted time.

Finally, when the time is up, be strict about stopping for your first checkpoint. You may need a whistle!

Step 7: Conduct a Checkpoint Review

At the end of each round stop and communicate each squad's status to the room. Do this by having a checkpoint: ask each squad to assess themselves against the skills checklist to indicate whether they have all the skills needed or if they are over- or undersubscribed in any area.

"Ten minutes," "Self-select," "Stop," "Announce to the room" is a pattern that has worked for us in every self-selection event, as depicted here.

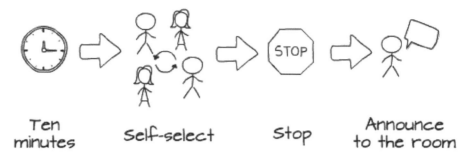

Ten
minutes   Self-select   Stop   Announce
                                       to the room

For your first checkpoint don't expect to have many fully formed squads. At this point it's okay to have empty squads, and you're likely to have many people in the "Not in a Squad" section.

The aim of the checkpoint is to set up squads to have constructive conversations during the next iteration and to make people aware of who should be talking to whom. During a checkpoint some squads may announce that they're missing a certain skill, while others might demonstrate an oversupply of the same.

Ask every squad to appoint a spokesperson to report back to the room. One by one the spokesperson from each squad should answer these questions:

- Is the squad fully formed?
- Are there any gaps in skills or numbers?
- Are there any problems or blocks?

Squad announcements often sound like these:

> This is Matt from the Bio Squad. We currently have too many developers, not enough testers, and no design.

> Brian from the Search Squad here. We don't have enough developers. We have too many testers, and we have four designers.

Any squad that is fully formed, that is, can deliver end to end, has all the skills needed, and fulfills the constraints, receives a check mark of approval (as shown in this image).

Members of approved squads remain in the room and take part in subsequent self-selection iterations. The fully formed squads' composition might still have to change and members move to other squads to make the bigger picture work. This doesn't happen very often, but it's good to keep the option open.

Try to move through each checkpoint as quickly as possible so that you can start the next round while you have momentum. More than likely the interesting conversations had just started when the timer sounded. You want to check in for direction, but focus on getting on with it.

Step 8: Rinse and Repeat

Repeat the ten-minute time slots, each followed by a checkpoint, as shown here, until all squads are fully formed or until you get to a point where people stop moving and you won't get any additional complete squads. (See When to Stop on page 55) for how you know when to stop and what to do next.)

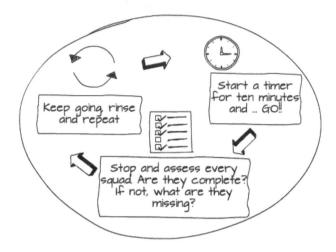

We don't recommend extending the time slot. However, it can be a good idea to make it shorter to speed things up if people look distracted, conversations aren't focused, or things are generally slowing down.

Facilitation

As a facilitator you should resist the urge to solve problems for people or lead them down a particular path. Asking open-ended questions and extending options is useful, but keep in mind that the ultimate squad design must come from the people involved and not you. This is why it's especially important that managers who aren't involved in actual hands-on squad work aren't present. If they're the type of people who dive in and take over—or even just stand at the back of the room getting frustrated—it will have a negative effect on the choices people make and ultimately endanger self-selection.

A good facilitator can make things a lot easier.

You will have to be alert for any sign that people aren't really self-selecting. At our largest squadification event we had to step in when a team lead started to direct people into squads based on where he thought the gaps were and who would have the most appropriate skills and seniority to fill them.

Sandy remembers:

> Our team leads are also parts of squads and do hands-on work. During our largest self-selection someone made us aware that the Business Analyst team lead was directing his people toward particular squads. I think he had good intentions, making sure the "right" person with the "right" skill set would be in the "right"

squad. We observed this guy trying to convince people to join a particular squad, and one conversation really bordered on coercion. We interfered with this situation immediately because as facilitators our primary job is to make sure that self-selection really is self-selection and that nobody can say afterward that they were influenced by their manager.

It takes three rounds

We've observed that every time we facilitate a self-selection event, it takes the group three rounds of ten-minute iterations to get the hang of things and to arrive at a solution or a point where more rounds won't get them any closer to a solution.

Usually round one is not very successful. People manage to create few fully formed squads, and most of the squads are either wildly over- or under-subscribed. For example, one of our first-round squads consisted of seven developers and no one else.

Round two is where things start to improve. This round usually results in more fully formed squads, but there still may be some over- and under-subscribed squads.

In round three the magic happens. People understand the process, they start talking, and squads begin to lobby for members. Negotiations and swaps happen, and some product owners or squad members reread the squad pitches to attract potential members.

When to Stop?

In our experience you'll come to a point after three or four rounds where more iterations won't be helpful. We recommend stopping when you either have all the squads you need—in which case congratulations are in order and you should send everyone home—or, if the problem isn't solved, engagement levels start dropping. In that case it's time to switch gears and tackle the outstanding problems by tweaking the format.

David recalls:

One of the things we wondered before Squadification Day was how we would know when to stop. How many squads are enough? On the big day we wanted eleven squads, but we knew five would be a good result. Seven would be even better. So, when should we stop during the day?

We weren't sure beforehand, but it turned out that the moment to stop was easy to recognize. When people started to chat with each other about the weather, about when the coffee was coming, and about other things that had nothing to do with their squads, we knew it was time to stop and assess where we were.

Step 9: Tackle the Outstanding Problems

There seems to be a point when all self-selection sessions reach an apparent stalemate. This often happens after three or four rounds. Most squads are complete, but one or two tricky ones still remain. This is the time to change in tactics rather than carrying on with more self-selection rounds.

You have several options for what you can do when you reach this point:

1. *Stop and call it a day. Take what you have as a win and solve the outstanding problems in a small group another day.*

   Following one of our self-selection events people went away overnight to think about the problem. While two hours of problem-solving time the day before hadn't led to a conclusion, several people realized overnight that the solution was staring them in the face: one developer switching squads would complete the puzzle. This hadn't been obvious because this particular person had worked in one area of the business for her whole time with the organization, and no one had thought of her moving.

2. *Hone in on your problems. Send people who are part of a fully formed squad home. Reducing the number of people involved lets you focus on creating the remaining squads.*

   Sometimes when squads aren't fully formed, the problem is easily identified and the solution is clear. However, the solution may require someone who has previously selected a squad to change or swap with someone else. This situation can create some tension if they don't want to change. This is where the reminder to "do what is best for your company" can be an effective tool to break the deadlock. In most cases participants will remind each other—in some cases literally pointing to the banner on the wall—and someone will act selflessly in this situation.

3. *Add imaginary people. Introduce "hire cards" and subsequently allow people to hire into their squads after the event.*

   One time we had a shortage of designers. No matter how we cut it, we just couldn't make any more fully formed squads. We could have thinly spread our designers across multiple squads, but that would have left every squad short and no one happy. As a group we decided instead to populate as many full squads as we could and then use empty index cards to represent the people we needed to hire after the event.

> ### A lens over your people
>
> People say scrum puts a lens over your business. In the same way, self-selection can put a lens over your staff, showing what skills you have too much and too little of. While this can be slightly uncomfortable, it's great information to have.

Try to create as many fully formed squads as possible—eight fully formed squads are a better result than eleven squads that are 90% complete.

We recommend pressing ahead as much as possible while you have momentum and the right people in the room. Just make sure that all decisions are really made by the group and not by you or any of the other facilitators.

Step 10: Wrap Up

Ideally after a few of rounds of self-selection you will have populated your new squads. Hopefully everyone has had a positive experience.

End your self-selection event by thanking people for their time and effort and by congratulating them on the results. Explain to everyone that you will document who is in which of the newly formed squads and that you'll be in touch about what's going to happen next. Let everyone know when they can expect the new squads to start.

Remember to take pictures of every squad diagram, including check marks of completeness and a record of any problems that remain to be solved. You'll need them to inform not only everyone who participated but also anyone who didn't participate in the event but is interested in the outcome, such as any managers you kicked out or asked not to come!

What Next?

This chapter provided you with a step-by-step guide for how to run your self-selection event. You now have a facilitation guide to follow with everything you need to know to run a successful event.

You learned about preparing the physical environment, setting the context for the day, running timed iterations, and collecting real-time feedback during checkpoints. You also received advice for when to stop running more iterations, and we provided you with options for how to tackle any outstanding problems.

Next we'll show you how to translate your squad blueprints into reality. You'll learn how to kick off your new squads as quickly as possible, respecting the spirit of self-selection and giving them the best possible chance of success.

After Self-Selection: Now What?

By now you will have successfully run your self-selection event. You've watched people react brilliantly to the level of trust you placed in them, and now you're faced with the job of making your squad diagrams real.

The question is, now what? In this chapter we explain the process and steps you need to take to make the outcomes of the self-selection event a reality and quickly and efficiently transition to your new structure.

Making It Real

At the end of a self-selection event, you usually end up with a lot of paper and hopefully a set of self-selected, fully skilled teams. But so far this information is just a collection of diagrams. You now need to go about making it real.

After the event, the participants often have a lot of questions about what's going to happen next, when they can start working in their new squads, and whether this is actually for real or if there will be some last-minute management decree that changes some of the teams that have been designed.

Protecting the outcome of your self-selection event is critical.

In the immediate aftermath following a self-selection event, it's crucial to confirm that this really is an accepted process and that everyone's choices will be respected. The organization needs to be aware that any change decreed or decision overruled by management will erode the foundation of trust and empowerment you just established, and in fact, the company would be left worse off than if you had used management selection from the beginning. Therefore, protecting the outcome of your self-selection event is critical.

The first thing to do is follow up with each of the newly formed squads. It's important to discuss ideas and concerns and, perhaps most important, to find a date members can start working together. We usually run a meeting with each of the squads using the Lean Coffee[1] format, which is a useful way to run an agenda-less meeting, where the topics for discussion are established by the squad itself. This allows us to manage expectations and to hand over responsibility to the squads to make it happen.

> ## Lean Coffee
>
> *Lean Coffee* is a structured but agenda-less meeting. It's a fast-paced, timed discussion where people get together, decide on an agenda, and start talking. A Lean Coffee starts with participants populating a kanban board with the topics or items they want to discuss. This forms the agenda and they discuss one item at a time for a set time. (We like three to five minutes.) Participants move a sticky note to "Doing" and discuss the topic before they move it to "Done."
>
> Once the time for that item expires, the group decides whether to keep discussing the topic and add another time slot or move on to the next topic. The meeting ends when the agreed time is up or when there are no more topics left to discuss.

You should meet with each new squad as soon as possible, ideally the very next day. It's vital that you build on the momentum you've created and don't let people go back to their regular jobs without closure from the self-selection event. You need to set the expectations for what will happen next.

You can expect some or all of these questions during these Lean Coffees:

- *When can we start and what happens to our current projects?*

  People are simply wondering "What now?" Do they continue with their current work? Do they need to finish it as fast as possible or hand it over to someone else?

- *Are we adequately resourced?*

  If there were any gaps in your newly created squads, people will be wondering how and when they will be filled. "Does everything we have established get put on hold until we recruit new people? This could take months!"

- *What about logistics?*

  For example, how will the seating arrangements be configured for the new squads? What are the time and date of the squad's first meeting?

---

1. http://www.leancoffee.org

It's a great sign of engagement when people are concerned about their current work and don't want to abandon existing projects. It would be a far more dire situation for the company if they didn't care at all. However, ongoing projects often create a web of dependencies where everything is dependent on everything else and there's no obvious place to start.

At Trade Me we were a bit like a tightly wound ball of string with no visible thread; we needed to cut into the ball to make a start. We had to consider the new hires who had been suggested as part of the selection process. Nobody wanted to wait for those people to arrive, but equally nobody wanted to start before the squad was fully skilled. In general we pursued the earliest starting point regardless of what talent were waiting for.

Kick squads off as early as possible. There will never be a perfect time, so if in doubt, go for sooner rather than later. Establish the new squads and let them cover for those who haven't started yet. It's not a big deal because it drives the kind of cross-functional "team-first" behavior you want to see.

Defining Squad Start Dates

It's important to create (and stick to) a schedule, especially if you have many squads, projects, and people. You get to choose whether to do this via a date-driven plan like a Gantt chart or a scope-based approach like a backlog of tasks. Don't let anyone drift, because you're likely to find some people will be frustrated waiting for their new squad to start and others will be gold-plating their existing project not knowing what comes next.

In our case we were dealing with a large organization with many ongoing projects, and we were growing rapidly. It took us almost two months to finish transitioning existing projects to the new squads. Among the contributing factors were unwieldy projects, Christmas holidays that happened to fall soon after, new recruits, and internal movements. We were constantly aware of the danger that until we had established the new squads, something could happen to stop or delay the formation of the new structure. This would have been a devastating blow to the people who had self-selected, so we worked hard to keep momentum. We recommend you do the same!

David says:

> Looking back, it was fascinating to see how those months were filled with little bursts of energy and enthusiasm when a new person arrived and a number of employees would be freed up and a number of squads could start. It felt a bit like when the perfect shape comes down in Tetris and we could fill three or four lines all at once.

It's helpful to make the timeline of your plan highly visible to everyone in the office. Display a large calendar with planned start times for squads and check them off and celebrate squads when they launch. We believe that transparency is an important part of keeping things going and not losing momentum.

One thing we didn't do in the beginning but have introduced to later events was regular follow-up meetings, usually every week, with the not-yet-formed squads to keep their focus and buy-in. Here people can raise whatever issue they like. It could be anything from dealing with change that inevitably comes along, such as "What are we going to do now that the project will take longer than we thought to complete?" to "What should we do now that the new hire won't start until four weeks later than we originally thought?" The answer is inevitably something those involved should decide, but the important thing is that squad members have the opportunity to voice their concerns and to creatively solve problems.

One main concern people often have is whether their squads are adequately resourced. Fundamentally, this is a sign that some squads don't feel confident that they're up to the task. It's understandable that they feel nervous and it's a natural part of any team formation. Reassure the squads that you trust their self-selection and that if they find after three months that they need another person or more of a particular skill, they'll be able to make the changes.

Kicking Off a New Squad

As things fall into place, you will often have new squads starting in rapid succession. You need to make sure that they're given the best possible start. After all, while the significant team-design part is now complete, 30% of a team's success will depend on how it's launched, as discussed in The Science Behind Team Design on page 4.

During self-selection people prove that they can be trusted to solve complex problems, know what's best for them and the company, and act as trusted adults. In the spirit of letting people control their way of working, we never mandate whether a squad should run scrum, kanban, their own special creation, or a traditional way of working. Following Daniel Pink's principles of motivation,[2] one of the key forms of autonomy is being in control of your processes. Giving people autonomy over who they work with should be extended by letting them choose how they work together.

---

2. http://www.ted.com/talks/dan_pink_on_motivation?language=en

It's important to maintain the spirit of self-selection and to ensure that squads understand that the trust and control they were given in designing their own squads isn't a one-off but an ongoing way of working. Truly high-performing squads need to be in control of the way they work. When our squads started, we guided them through a process of selecting agile and lean practices to help them come up with a system that worked for them.

Who Should Be There?

The entire squad. If someone can't make it, find a different date—it's really important that everyone have a say in how the squad is going to work.

There should be a facilitator with enough agile experience to facilitate a discussion around when to use scrum, when to use kanban, and the purpose and meaning of each agile practice. An agile coach would be ideal, but others with the same knowledge would work too.

How Much Time Do We Need?

Depending on team size and personalities, reserve somewhere between a couple of hours and a day.

What Do We Do?

Part 1: Get to Know Each Other (One–Two Hours)

For the team to work well together in the future, they need to establish connections while building trust and understanding for each other. We recommend using an exercise such as Lyssa Adkins's "Journey Lines" as a starting point. This exercise has proved to be one of the best team-building activities we've experienced.

Journey Lines involve people drawing a graph that represents the journey of their career and/or private lives. People draw along two axes, one of time and and one of happiness. They're free to share as much or as little as they're comfortable with. You can find additional detail and instructions for this exercise in Lyssa Adkins's excellent book *Coaching Agile Teams*. [Adk10]

Part 2: Choose Your Agile Ingredients (One Hour)

In this part the squad defines how they will work, including which elements of agile they will use. We start off with the squad generating a list of agile ingredients and practices they know from scrum, kanban, XP, or anything else. Participants simply shout out the practices, and the facilitator writes them on a whiteboard to create a list of options.

This is what squads normally come up with (if your squad doesn't, you can use this as a starter list to bring up yourself):

- Sprints (If so, how long?)
- Kanban workflow
- Explicitly limit WIP
- Coordination: daily standup
- Feedback process: retrospectives
- Visual workspace
- Measure/track velocity? cycle time? lead time?
- Planning: sprint planning? on demand or on a regular basis?
- Backlog refinement sessions
- Forecasting, product burnup charts, burndown charts
- Sprint reviews (demonstrations)
- Test-driven development, specification by example
- Coordination with other squads: scrum of scrums
- Have an agile coach

Next it's important to discuss each practice/ingredient and decide what the team will choose to use or experiment with. The purpose of this is to further develop the understanding of these practices with members making active choices about how they will work—as opposed to blindly following a process.

For any practice the squad decides not to do, ask how else the practice's purpose will be achieved. For example, if a squad decides not to have stand-up meetings, they'll need to decide how they'll meet the aim of that practice—coordination.

There are two agile practices we believe should remain mandatory: retrospectives and physical story walls (if you are co-located). Retrospectives are key because they drive continuous improvement; deciding not to keep a retrospective is like saying "We don't want to get better." Physical story walls are important, particularly to new squads, because they act as a focal point for conversations. While a new squad may not yet be ready for healthy conflict, the presence of a board allows the important issues to be visualized—and people can have those healthy discussions around the board.

Part 3: Decide on the Practical Stuff (Thirty Minutes–One Hour)

Once you've decided which practices to follow, it's time to deal with the practical matters. These will include the squad's definition of "done," the length of sprints, and the time and day meetings will take place. The squad should also decide which tools it will use or those it will experiment with as a starting point.

Supporting Squads

We mentioned earlier in The Science Behind Team Design on page 4 that J. Richard Hackman's research indicates that the remaining 10% of team performance (in addition to the 60% attributed to team design and 30% to the way the team is launched) is attributable to how the team is supported once it's under way. This kind of leader-coaching support should surround the team, and it should include line managers, agile coaches, and mentors.

Assign an agile coach to support and educate each new squad; a coach can also offer further training and have regular check points with each new squad throughout the early months. In our case at Trade Me, we were constrained by the number of full-time agile coaches available, so we worked on growing internal knowledge and support. When people had been part of successful squads for a number of months, the knowledge and experience they had built up meant they would be perfectly placed to support our future teams, and we were establishing a train-the-trainer model almost without knowing it.

However you choose to support your squads, the important thing is to make yourself and others available and able to offer support, guidance, and challenge when necessary.

What Not To Do

Great learning often comes from failure, and there are certainly several mistakes we have made or observed in others.

One of our business areas followed up their self-selection event with a management call to move one person from their selected squad. This is something still talked about in the hallways and brought up in the run-up to any scheduled self-selection event. We use this example to demonstrate what can go wrong, if after all the good intentions of a self-selection event people can't resist the urge to dive in, solve problems on others' behalf, and move people around by management selection. It was obvious to everyone that this completely undermined the process that we had followed, and there was a combination of sympathy for the people highlighted to be moved and anger toward those doing the moving. We can't stress enough that self-selection isn't just a one-off event but a set of principles that should be followed indefinitely.

We said previously that the only thing worse than managerial selection is a fake self-selection where people are led to believe they're in charge of their own destiny, only to find out that wasn't the case at all. It's important to stick to your guns and follow through on the principles on which you promised the event to your participants.

This is also worth taking into account for future hiring, which should directly involve the squad. It would be wrong to ignore the process of self-selection and choosing squads by hiring a new employee and plunking that person into a squad without considering what people want or need.

What Next?

We covered what to do immediately after a self-selection event and how to kick off the new squads in a way that will give them the best possible chance of success. We made a case for establishing your squads as quickly as possible and for being transparent with the squad start dates. We also left you with some warnings of what not to do. In the next chapter we share key insights into people's behavior and experiences during self-selection.

Insights

We've facilitated many self-selection events in various locations and have talked to several other companies that have followed the principles and our process for self-selection. We've observed a number of patterns that emerge almost every time—patterns that we believe are fundamental to self-selection. In this chapter we share key insights into people's behavior and experiences during self-selection.

People Appreciate Self-Selection

After each self-selection event we've been part of, participant feedback has been incredibly positive. Almost everyone is in favor of self-selection as the best way to design teams. Even those who initially fear and doubt the process come away with a positive attitude. Participants tell us they're surprised by how productive and valuable they found the process, especially after admitting they were initially skeptical about its potential for success.

Most people like the squad they end up being a part of. Even those who may not be entirely happy with the end result fully understand and appreciate the reasons why they're on the squad they are because they were part of the conversation and the process. Contrast that to those finding out they've been assigned a new squad by management selection and you can understand the different reaction self-selection generates. A number of people also tell us that they now work on the squad they expected to work on before the event took place, so participants seem to go into the day with a certain level of expectation about how the process will pan out.

At the end of every event we always ask everyone about their experiences and whether their expectations have been met. We also ask what they think of the process and whether they appreciate the results it generated. What follows is a sample of the survey we use to ask participants for their feedback.

POST SELF-SELECTION PARTICIPANT SURVEY

☐ 1. How did you find the experience of self-selection?

☐ 2. Did you end up on the squad you thought you would?

☐ 3. Are you happy with the squad you will be on?

☐ 4. What primarily drove your self-selection choices?
- ☐ Type of work
- ☐ Product owner
- ☐ Doing what was best for the company
- ☐ People you did want to work with
- ☐ People you did not want to work with
- ☐ Other (please tell us)

☐ 5. What did you particularly like about self-selection?

☐ 6. What did you particularly dislike about self-selection?

☐ 7. Would you recommend others follow this model?

☐ 8. Tell us one thing you observed during the event.

☐ 9. Any other thoughts, suggestions, or observations?

The survey is a combination of questions scored on a scale of 1 to 5 that give us insight into what participants think and other questions that give us a kind of Net Promoter Score (question 7).[1] We also include open questions so people can respond freely. We usually gain excellent insights from the open questions. Here are some of our favorite quotes from past surveys:

- *"Freedom! Fascinating to see how it all worked out. Excellent result, and nice to know we were able to achieve it without having to get dictatorial."*

- *"It was a good way to bring issues to the fore quickly and show them visually. I kind of liked going round and seeing whether squads were formed or not."*

- *"It did give people the chance to choose where they wanted to go, but everyone was also thinking about what would work best for the company."*

---

1.   https://en.wikipedia.org/wiki/Net_Promoter

- *"I did not observe tension or conflict, which was a great thing. Proved that this was a valuable exercise."*

- *"Got to chat with people I'd only seen around the office but not really met yet. Also the fact that we actually get to do this at all. Would never even have been considered in my last company."*

At the self-selection event at Trade Me, it was interesting to notice that people in their thirties and forties, who had been in the workforce longer than others, had much more awareness of what a privilege the opportunity to self-select was (especially when compared to recent graduates). People working in their first jobs probably assume this is normal, and hopefully, with their expectations being met and such a positive experience, it soon will be!

Relationships Are the Deciding Factor

Across the different self-selection events we've been part of, it's been fascinating to observe what people base their squad selection on. The most important factor we've seen has been their personal relationships—participants make decisions almost exclusively based on who they want to work with—and in some cases who they don't want to work with. That said, it can be hard for people to admit up front or even after the fact that they based their decision on their relationships with others. They seem to feel that the correct answer is the type of work or the opportunity for learning. Perhaps that's the kind of thing people have had drilled into them since early in their career.

In a survey we conducted after our largest self-selection event, most people told us they had based their decision exclusively on doing what was best for the company and/or the type of work they wanted to do. But that ran contrary to all our observations. During the events most of the conversations we overhear are about who wants to work with whom, and we noticed that many people were only available in groups (or mini-teams) of two or three. Often when one person moved, we saw other people move along with them or very soon after.

Those who had not been able to make it to the event through absence or sickness nominated proxies to make a selection on their behalf. The most frequent instruction to proxies was "Make sure I'm in your/their squad."

It's fair to say that sometimes employees don't want to work with each other. And that's okay. People know whether they're going to gel in a squad with a particular person, and if not, it makes sense they would choose not to work with him or her. This process, unlike management selection, allows them to make that choice.

At our first self-selection event we observed two participants in particular who seemed to have taken a real dislike to each other. When one of them moved his photograph to a squad the other one was in, the second person immediately moved his photo to a different squad. This happened several times, and whenever those two ended up in the same squad, one of them would quickly move again. This wasn't a problem at all; there wasn't any drama, and those affected made a choice that was good for them and their squads. Had they been selected to work together, as they easily could have been by managers focusing only on compatible skills, both they and their squads would have suffered.

People Respond Well to This Level of Trust

We originally went into large-scale self-selection with considerable fear of the consequences and worries about how people would respond. However, we can now categorically state that none of our fears were justified. Our concerns didn't become reality, and with the benefit of hindsight, we were worked up over nothing. Given this unprecedented level of trust, individuals acted professionally and as responsible adults.

There was no reason to believe that this kind of exercise would bring out any of the bad behavior we and others had originally feared. In fact, one of the greatest wins of following a process like this was to see that employees demonstrated that they really can be trusted to solve complex problems in a way that's best for the organization.

With the benefit of hindsight, David remembers the scenario after we had carried out our biggest event:

> So, we went through a really fascinating experiment. It was just so interesting to watch what participants did during the entire process. Overall, we were really pleasantly surprised that it just seemed to work. On one hand, we felt really lucky because people had jumped into this process, acted like trusted colleagues, and behaved incredibly well throughout the whole thing. Importantly, they really enjoyed it as well!

> On the other hand, maybe it wasn't luck because what we had done was trust and empower people and then step aside to see the incredible results. The whole process just seems to work really well for everyone. It has been so much better to see everyone solve the puzzle themselves rather than to have me, or anybody else, tell them what they should and shouldn't be doing.

> On that day, the participants definitely won. On that day and afterward, everyone just seemed happier. In fact, we actively measure the happiness of the staff, and we know that things improved significantly after that day. They're now working in

their stable squads, working with whom they want to work with and on the type of work they want to do. That's something we're very proud of indeed.

Employees in squads who had the privilege to decide for themselves whom they wanted to work with weren't the only winners. The company learned a lot about what people actually wanted to do. This information will be highly relevant for recruitment in the future. For example, after the first selection round, almost all developers had moved themselves into squads focusing on back-end–heavy projects, leaving the more front-end and design-centric squads. So we could see we had a weight of interest in certain areas and not in others.

The management team, which wasn't directly involved in the process, of course, found the feedback to be incredibly useful, even when that feedback highlighted areas of the company as less appealing to work in. It provided a great opportunity to dig deeper and to ask the right questions.

After a self-selection event at his company, Roger Nesbitt, development manager at Powershop NZ, said:

> *We learned that our delivery team staff have a deep understanding of what makes a good team and the self-discipline to organize themselves. Looking at the teams that were self-selected, we (as managers) couldn't think of a better arrangement of people and skills.*

A key difference between self-selection and managerial selection is that with self-selection people understand why certain decisions or compromises have been made. Even if tough calls are required, they understand why and will have been involved in the decisions. When new squads are established via self-selection, a very different environment emerges from one in which coworkers question or misunderstand key decisions that have been made by managers above them. Self-selection might seem tiring, slow, or even frustrating at the time, but the process is as important as the outcome.

What Next?

The insights shared here have been common to each of the self-selection events we have run. People really enjoy the process, they tend to make decisions based almost exclusively on relationships, and they respond incredibly well to this level of trust.

Next we move on to look at the long-term effects of self-selection, using our case studies, measurements, and examples to demonstrate what has happened in the months and years following self-selection events.

CHAPTER 7

Long-Term Effects of Self-Selection

The real benefits of self-selection at Trade Me did not emerge in the short term. Yes, people were happy on the day itself and for the weeks that followed, but the positive effects were mainly realized over the long term.

It's now a number of years after the company's first foray into self-selection, and we're in a position to share with you the impact it has had on employees, squads, and the wider organization. In fact, self-selection has been so successful that it has become the default method by which teams are created as the company continues to scale.

In some cases we know Trade Me has attracted people to join solely as a result of self-selection. "Is it really true that people get to choose whom they work with here?" became a common question at recruitment events.

The company continues to grow in size and revenue, and while it might be hard to measure the direct impact of self-selection on the company's stock price and bottom line, there are a number of areas that we could measure directly and track against our work in order to draw conclusions. In this chapter we demonstrate how employee happiness increased, stress levels dropped, and productivity rose above and beyond our expectations.

The Effect on Happiness

When our journey started several years ago, employees were feeling stressed and we could feel the frustration in the air as we walked around the office. Speaking to coworkers would often bring tales of disappointment and irritation.

Since we were embarking on unchartered territory with self-selection, we knew that we needed to have measurements in place that would tell us if we were heading in the right direction and whether the effects would wear off over time, having provided a temporary spike only.

Measuring happiness is not an exact science, but you can to gather samples and track trends over time. In our case we designed and built a tool that we referred to as the Happiness, Innovation, and Productivity (HIP) survey.

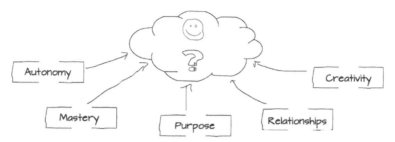

The HIP survey is our take on how to gain information on how healthy our work environment is and how we're doing in creating a place that fosters happiness, innovation, and productivity. The survey questions build on Daniel Pink's work on autonomy, mastery, and purpose as described on page 6 and the Scandinavian Workplace Happiness movement (*arbejdsglæde*),[1] which adds relationships and creativity to the mix.

The checklist that follows shows some of the most important motivational factors we collect information on, as listed in the survey that follows:

HAPPINESS, INNOVATION, AND PRODUCTIVITY SURVEY

On a scale of 1-5, to what degree do you feel you...

- ☐ Are doing meaningful work that comes to fruition on our website/applications? (Purpose)

- ☐ Are allowed to do what's best for your work by focusing on one thing at a time? (Creativity)

- ☐ Have direct influence on how we work and solve problems? (Autonomy)

- ☐ Work in a squad where people support and challenge each other? (Relationships)

- ☐ Have been able to learn new skills at work? (Mastery)

- ☐ Can be creative at work through success and failure? (Creativity)

Is there anything specific that has affected your scores?

---

1. http://www.whattheheckisarbejdsglaede.com

Over time we saw the happiness levels trend upward in all of these areas. Like any trend, the development wasn't perfectly even; we observed peaks and troughs, particularly around the introduction of new squads, difficult projects, or the financial end of year.

The following graphs illustrate the results we observed from the questions in the HIP survey.

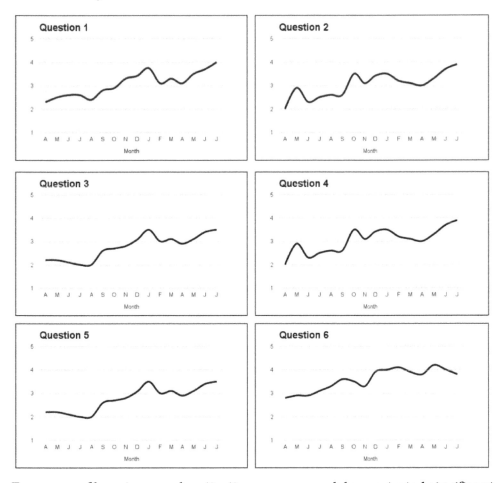

Every area of happiness and motivation we measured demonstrated significant improvement over time. Levels of autonomy, mastery, purpose, and creativity increased, and employees found they received more support from those around them. We also measured a reduction in multitasking, which increased our focus and productivity.

The Effect on Squads

We've seen fewer personality clashes and petty disagreements in our squads. In fact, many have become so tightly knit that they have become known as "work families" with bonds extending well beyond their agile meetings and daily collaboration.

Squads at Trade Me have also become far more stable.

Before our first self-selection, one of the most common concerns was that participants would be "signing away their lives," having to work on a squad for as long as they were with the company. Not only did this concern turn out to be unfounded, but people seem to be going to great lengths to remain with their current squads.

When we were faced with this concern in the very beginning, we promised the option to have re-squadifications every six months. In reality, though, the only time people have taken us up on that offer has been when the company's growth was so significant that it drove new choices, rather than team members reconsidering whether their initial self-selection choice was the right one.

If your company grows by more than 25%, it will most likely be a good idea to ask people to re-squadify. After all, it might not make sense to have a bunch of newbies form an all-new squad, and it would be unfair to those who joined the company because of the prospect of self-selection.

The Effect on Managers

As a result of spending less time selecting teams, moving employees around based on short-term resource needs, and mediating petty disagreements between coworkers, the role of managers has changed significantly after self-selection.

Managers no longer have to maintain a constant state of readiness to solve personnel problems. Rather than constantly escalating issues, squads now solve their own problems, and managers have the time and energy to think and plan for the future and to focus on strategic decisions. They're able to provide real leadership, as opposed to just management, and to help their staff in their growth, development, and career planning.

> ### The transition can be difficult
>
> One manager described his former way of working as that of a meerkat—pop up, look around, find a fire to fight. He was so used to this way of working that for weeks he'd still pop up, look around, realize there was no fire for him to fight, and sit down again. Moving to a more strategic and proactive position can be a reasonably difficult transition, but a highly rewarding one nonetheless.

The Effect on Productivity

Overall our measurements didn't just tell us that employees were happier and teams more stable; they also showed that the company's delivery was significantly faster and of higher quality than before self-selection.

Measuring productivity in software development is difficult, and as far as we can tell, no one has discovered the perfect measure. Our way of understanding and tracking overall productivity was driven by finding measures that may not be perfect but drive the right behaviors. Therefore, we chose to focus on the following metrics:

- *Throughput*: the number of user stories shipped within a time period

- *Cycle time*: the time from when work begins on a request to when it is deployed to end users

- *Quality*: the number of bugs on production and failure demand, that is, work necessary to correct errors and shortcomings

The company's average cycle time was cut in half over the course of a year and quality measures also indicated significant improvements.

One measure of productivity was the total number of user stories shipped.

While we knew these were measures that could be gamed and manipulated, we had chosen them specifically for this particular reason: Most people will attempt to "game" any metrics or key performance indicators (KPIs) they are presented with, and gaming these metrics will bring positive outcomes.

Slicing features into smaller user stories and releasing to production more often—for example, to increase throughput numbers—would generate only positive outcomes. It would only increase our ability to generate value early and lower the risk of building big features.

Since self-selection we've seen a significant rise in the number of user stories shipped to production. Our hypothesis that stable squads made up of people who had chosen to work together would be more productive proved to be true. The days of disbanding squads at the end of a project just as they were starting to work well together or disbanding them because we, as managers, had gotten the team composition wrong seemed a long way behind us.

Of course, improving productivity doesn't create success; it's possible to run fast in the wrong direction after all. We saw more features being released and also more products and improvements that users loved. It wasn't all about getting stuff out the door, though, because the healthier our squads became, the more they would collaborate with the product owners. They would often have new feature ideas, question the value of prioritized features, or find new and innovative ways to test concepts early.

As discussed earlier in the section Today's Work Demands Stable Teams on page 1, research by Rally Software showed that stable teams are up to 60% more productive. Our company saw similar results, and our throughput doubled over the course of the first year.

The Effect on the Company

The first year after the initial self-selection event, Trade Me posted record results with revenue up 13% year-on-year (not that we're laying claim to this as any sort of expected gain!). Since then, we have continued to expand, adding more squads and more people. At last count the total number of squads was approaching forty, with the number of people involved in product development rising to 300.

As a company listed on the stock exchange and with demanding stakeholders, Trade Me's desire to grow and add new features is unlikely to decrease. Working in stable squads and empowering people to make good decisions for themselves has added to an already strong company culture. It has also had the unlikely side effect of people explicitly joining the company in order to choose what they work on and whom they work with.

Now It's Your Turn

Self-selection honors the principle of trusting people to solve complex problems and stepping back to enable them to organize in the way that's best for themselves and the organization. We believe that companies can get the best results when people choose what they work on and who they work with.

Now it's your turn to go and do it, to try self-selection and test your own hypotheses and find the best way to work for your organization. We hope this book has given you the impetus, the tools, and the insight to do so. In addition, you may find these resources useful as you dive head first into self-selection:

- Everything for self-selection http://nomad8.com/category/self-selection/

- Self-Selection Kit http://nomad8.com/team-self-selection-kit/

- How we measure work happiness http://nomad8.com/how-we-measure-work-happiness/

- The blog from our first self-selection experiment http://nomad8.com/the-self-organising-organisation/

- The blog from our largest self-selection event http://nomad8.com/total-squadification-large-scale-self-organisation/

- How MYOB in Australia got on following our process http://nomad8.com/self-selection-in-90-minutes-interview-with-simon-alex-from-myob/

- How Australia Post got on following our process http://nomad8.com/large-scale-self-selection-at-australia-post-interview-with-andy-kelk/

- How we kick off new squads http://nomad8.com/how-we-kick-off-new-squads/

- How we measure productivity http://nomad8.com/measure-output-and-productivity/

What Would You Do If You Weren't Afraid?

We hope you now feel ready, but bear in mind that it will never be the perfect time to do this. You will never fully clear the decks and get all your projects to a perfect state of completion, so maybe it's time to jump right in.

After all, you can ask yourself the question we posed to each other early on: what would you do if you weren't afraid?

Bibliography

[Adk10]   Lyssa Adkins. *Coaching Agile Teams: A Companion for ScrumMasters, Agile Coaches, and Project Managers in Transition*. Addison-Weslcy Professional, Boston, MA, 2010.

[Hac02]   J. Richard Hackman. *Leading Teams: Setting the Stage for Great Performances*. Harvard University Press, Boston, MA, 2002.

[McK95]   Leo McKinstry. *Lancaster: The Second World War's Greatest Bomber*. John Murray, London, UK, 20095.

[Pin09]   Daniel H. Pink. *Drive: The Surprising Truth About What Motivates Us*. Riverhead Books, New York, NY, USA, 2009.

Pragmatic Programming

We'll show you how to be more pragmatic and effective, for new code and old.

Your Code as a Crime Scene

Jack the Ripper and legacy codebases have more in common than you'd think. Inspired by forensic psychology methods, this book teaches you strategies to predict the future of your codebase, assess refactoring direction, and understand how your team influences the design. With its unique blend of forensic psychology and code analysis, this book arms you with the strategies you need, no matter what programming language you use.

Adam Tornhill
(218 pages) ISBN: 9781680500387. $36
https://pragprog.com/book/atcrime

The Nature of Software Development

You need to get value from your software project. You need it "free, now, and perfect." We can't get you there, but we can help you get to "cheaper, sooner, and better." This book leads you from the desire for value down to the specific activities that help good Agile projects deliver better software sooner, and at a lower cost. Using simple sketches and a few words, the author invites you to follow his path of learning and understanding from a half century of software development and from his engagement with Agile methods from their very beginning.

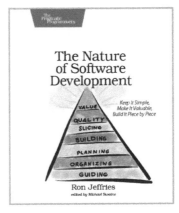

Ron Jeffries
(178 pages) ISBN: 9781941222379. $24
https://pragprog.com/book/rjnsd

Past and Present

To see where we're going, remember how we got here, and learn how to take a healthier approach to programming.

Fire in the Valley

In the 1970s, while their contemporaries were protesting the computer as a tool of dehumanization and oppression, a motley collection of college dropouts, hippies, and electronics fanatics were engaged in something much more subversive. Obsessed with the idea of getting computer power into their own hands, they launched from their garages a hobbyist movement that grew into an industry, and ultimately a social and technological revolution. What they did was invent the personal computer: not just a new device, but a watershed in the relationship between man and machine. This is their story.

Michael Swaine and Paul Freiberger
(424 pages) ISBN: 9781937785765. $34
https://pragprog.com/book/fsfire

The Healthy Programmer

To keep doing what you love, you need to maintain your own systems, not just the ones you write code for. Regular exercise and proper nutrition help you learn, remember, concentrate, and be creative—skills critical to doing your job well. Learn how to change your work habits, master exercises that make working at a computer more comfortable, and develop a plan to keep fit, healthy, and sharp for years to come.

This book is intended only as an informative guide for those wishing to know more about health issues. In no way is this book intended to replace, countermand, or conflict with the advice given to you by your own healthcare provider including Physician, Nurse Practitioner, Physician Assistant, Registered Dietician, and other licensed professionals.

Joe Kutner
(254 pages) ISBN: 9781937785314. $36
https://pragprog.com/book/jkthp

Explore Testing and Cucumber

Explore the uncharted waters of exploratory testing and beef up your automated testing with more Cucumber—now for Java, too.

Explore It!

Uncover surprises, risks, and potentially serious bugs with exploratory testing. Rather than designing all tests in advance, explorers design and execute small, rapid experiments, using what they learned from the last little experiment to inform the next. Learn essential skills of a master explorer, including how to analyze software to discover key points of vulnerability, how to design experiments on the fly, how to hone your observation skills, and how to focus your efforts.

Elisabeth Hendrickson
(186 pages) ISBN: 9781937785024. $29
https://pragprog.com/book/ehxta

The Cucumber for Java Book

Teams working on the JVM can now say goodbye forever to misunderstood requirements, tedious manual acceptance tests, and out-of-date documentation. Cucumber—the popular, open-source tool that helps teams communicate more effectively with their customers—now has a Java version, and our bestselling *Cucumber Book* has been updated to match. *The Cucumber for Java Book* has the same great advice about how to deliver rock-solid applications collaboratively, but with all code completely rewritten in Java. New chapters cover features unique to the Java version of Cucumber, and reflect insights from the Cucumber team since the original book was published.

Seb Rose, Matt Wynne & Aslak Hellesoy
(338 pages) ISBN: 9781941222294. $36
https://pragprog.com/book/srjcuc

The Pragmatic Bookshelf

The Pragmatic Bookshelf features books written by developers for developers. The titles continue the well-known Pragmatic Programmer style and continue to garner awards and rave reviews. As development gets more and more difficult, the Pragmatic Programmers will be there with more titles and products to help you stay on top of your game.

Visit Us Online

This Book's Home Page
https://pragprog.com/book/mmteams
Source code from this book, errata, and other resources. Come give us feedback, too!

Register for Updates
https://pragprog.com/updates
Be notified when updates and new books become available.

Join the Community
https://pragprog.com/community
Read our weblogs, join our online discussions, participate in our mailing list, interact with our wiki, and benefit from the experience of other Pragmatic Programmers.

New and Noteworthy
https://pragprog.com/news
Check out the latest pragmatic developments, new titles and other offerings.

Save on the eBook

Save on the eBook versions of this title. Owning the paper version of this book entitles you to purchase the electronic versions at a terrific discount.

PDFs are great for carrying around on your laptop—they are hyperlinked, have color, and are fully searchable. Most titles are also available for the iPhone and iPod touch, Amazon Kindle, and other popular e-book readers.

Buy now at *https://pragprog.com/coupon*

Contact Us

Online Orders:	*https://pragprog.com/catalog*
Customer Service:	*support@pragprog.com*
International Rights:	*translations@pragprog.com*
Academic Use:	*academic@pragprog.com*
Write for Us:	*http://write-for-us.pragprog.com*
Or Call:	+1 800-699-7764